T5-AFC-076

Another Dance of Life

The Aftermath of War

Another Dance of Life

The Aftermath of War

*For the Westerly Library +
Wilcox Park:
where I spent many a
happy hour.*

Helen H. Buchholtz

Helen H. Buchholtz

Old Mountain Press

3 4858 00317 5453

Published by:
Old Mountain Press, Inc.
2542 S. Edgewater Dr.
Fayetteville, NC 28303

www.oldmountainpress.com

Copyright © 2003 Helen H. Buchholtz

ISBN: 1-931575-31-2
Library of Congress Control Number: 2003094739

Another Dance of Life: The Aftermath of War
All rights reserved. Except for brief excerpts used in reviews, no portion of this work may be reproduced or published without expressed written permission from the author or the author's agent.

First Edition
Printed and bound in the United States of America by Morris Publishing •
www.morrispublishing.com • 800-650-7888
1 2 3 4 5 6 7 8 9 10

CONTENTS

Preface
and
Acknowledgments

This book is dedicated to my loving husband Stan, who helped edit and promote my first book, *American Hamburger–An American Girl in Nazi Germany*, which received a second prize from The National League of American Pen Women.

To all those displaced and homeless on the planet, may you find peaceful neighbors who appreciate this miracle Earth.

The horrendous terrorist attacks of 9/11 sent an immediate panic signal through my body. I thought all of my WWII experiences of fear, helplessness, and despair had been brought under control. Watching the TV replays, and listening to the radio reports awakened the emotions of anger at the perpetrators foremost, and empathy for the victims and their families. I found myself shaking as when I had cowered in air raid shelters during the Allied raids on the city of Hamburg.

My heart goes out to all victims who find themselves in zones of conflict, threatened by terrorists of religious or ethnic ideologies. Let us unite to preserve this precious planet. I fervently hope that my experiences will, in some small measure at least, awaken the innate desire of my readers to be proactive in achieving world unity. My own family's involvement with the Friendship Force promoted by Jimmy and Rosalyn Carter in acting as hosts to Korean visitors, and as ambassadors to Hannover , Germany, is one of our ways of contributing. Another is our active promotion of the international auxiliary language Esperanto, which we hope will become a major factor in furthering understanding between the peoples of the world.

Displaced

British Air Marshal Arthur Travers (Bomber) Harris had planned to destroy and demoralize the workforce of Hamburg, annihilating residential as well as industrial buildings under *Operation Gomorrah*, from July 25th to August 3rd, 1943.

It is a miracle that we survived this gigantic onslaught. 3000 aircraft dumped more than 9000 tons of deadly cargo on the city, resulting in a huge fire storm with hurricane type winds. The wind force twisted 25–30 year old trees like match sticks. One third of all residential houses, 24 hospitals, 277 schools, and 58 churches were completely destroyed.

31,647 dead were found by search and rescue up to November of that year; only half could be identified. Of the previous 800,000 ration cards originally distributed, approximately 62,000 fewer residents remained to claim their new ration cards.

The most important lesson I learned during the devastating bombing of Hamburg, was the pressing need for water. We nearly succumbed from the lack of it. Adequate water is essential to every living cell to regulate chemical processes in the human body. The outside scaffolding of the air raid bunker which we habituated, as well as adjacent buildings, streets, and even the asphalt were ablaze, causing a huge inferno. We lay on the floor in darkness, listening to the crackling flames, with the light of the fire glaring through the smoky haze of the unfinished porthole windows.

"Water, water," I groaned, which then turned into a mute chorus in my mind. One of the old block wardens braved leaving the shelter in search of the precious liquid. He returned after several hours, with the morning sun trying to penetrate the portholes through a poisonous yellow-green vapor. The meager ration allotted each of us was a handkerchief dip into the pail of murky water. I sucked on my share until it was dry. We all were soot-covered from the debris entering the openings. "Let's leave to try to find water and your father!" my mother whispered.

Not that I actually realized it at the time, but when we survived the terrible bombing of the city, it was already the fourth epic change of my life. The happy Manhattan era, from the time of my birth in the German section of New York City, to the move to Long Island, was like a Hollywood movie to me. Fortunately, the crisis of the great depression did not deprive us of food, shelter, clothing, or recreation. My father, and his brother Hans, and most of their merchant seaman friends had always found employment. My mother, and my uncle's wife Grete, were good household managers, using those skills in their own homes, as well as taking on additional outside work in apartment house management, or in child care for the wealthy.

On weekends, holidays, or duty free time, we frequented the movies, Central Park, the museums, ice cream parlors, cafes, Horn & Hardart automats, and Madison Square Garden. Automobile or motorcycle trips plotted to Connecticut, New Jersey, Washington, D.C., and the Skyline Drive of Virginia were the furthest we ventured out of the great New York metropolis at that time. Papa and Uncle Hans did all the tinkering with their cars because gas stations and repair shops were not as numerous as today. Cars and motorcycles were not that reliable in those days, so that most men depended on their own mechanical skills to maintain their vehicles. They could repair most problems in the backyard, on New York City streets, and along the country roads. My father once even repaired his Harley on an oilcloth stretched out over the living room rug.

The move out of the city to Hicksville, Long Island, was lamented by Uncle Hans as a most foolhardy idea. "You, who, like me, has jumped ship, will regret leaving New York City," he would repeatedly comment. I, of course, had this romantic picture in my mind of handsome sailors leaping from ocean liners onto the New

York piers. What could possibly be ominous with that thought? However, when my father bought a piece of land in Bethpage, designed, planned, and worked on the completion of our new house, the stress on him became excessive. He had been commuting to New York City on his motorcycle to his night manager job at Gracie Square. He would return home in the mornings as I boarded the yellow school bus, and immediately plunge into the labors of mitering, hanging doors, or installing cabinets. For weeks, he had kept up that grueling routine, with the disastrous outcome of a mental as well as physical breakdown. A doctor was called. Unfortunately, as we later discovered, this doctor was prejudiced towards Germans, and learning of my father's illegal status through his feverish murmurings, notified the immigration authorities. A few days later, as I stepped off the Bethpage school bus, I saw a large, black limo parked in our yard. Hoping it would be Uncle Hans, whom we had not seen for some time since we had moved to Bethpage, I ran to the house. As I passed by the limo, I read the lettering *Immigration and Naturalization Services* on the side of the vehicle. This bureau, my mother later explained to me, inspects the papers of all persons arriving in every American port of entry. It admits or rejects aliens, and may deport any persons having entered the country illegally. I knew that my father and his brother had become seamen for the express purpose of trying to find the whereabouts of their own father, who had left their home in Kiel, Germany, for the United States when they were children. They had never learned of the ultimate fate of their father. The final result of the discovery of my father's status was that he was to be returned to Germany to apply for documentation for legal reentry to the U.S.A.

My mother was given the option of applying for welfare support during my father's absence to sustain us. She vehemently declined this offer, and decided to accompany him to Hamburg. With a cheerful front, Mama said to me, "You will meet your German relatives, and we will be back in America within a few months. We will sail aboard the S.S. Roosevelt, the Presidential Line to Ireland, England, France, and Germany."

Going to sea like my father, uncle, and their merchant seamen friends had, cheered me. I recalled all of these events after having survived the horrendous fire bombing of Hamburg. When will this war end, and will we survive it?

What to do with the Homeless

The first place we each had agreed upon to look in case of separation was our house location.

When we arrived there, what we found to our great dismay, was nothing more than smoldering piles of rubble throughout the entire neighborhood. We decided to look for water down by the river, and found a makeshift Red Cross station set up there. The Elbe River block warden directed all the gathered homeless to a paddle wheel ferry, which took us down river to Blankenese, a suburb of Hamburg. There, locals who had been urged by the authorities to agree to take in bombed-out victims, met us , and we were taken in by a very kind lady. We stayed at Frau Henze's home for ten days. Each day, my mother returned to the city to visit our home site in the hope of finding some message. On the eighth day, she found a small pyramid with a hand written note secured by a stone. The note had been written by a neighbor at the direction of my father, informing her that he was in a field hospital being treated for temporary blindness induced by the incendiary bombs. Mama then arranged to have him brought to Frau Henze's house, where my mother carefully bathed his eye hourly. Our concern for his eye was great, due to the fact that his other eye had already been lost in a childhood accident.

Papa had two good days of rest in the Henze household to recover. The following morning, we reported to the designated building which the Blankenese warden had ordered us to. If we had not complied, our ration cards would not have been approved. Without ration cards, it would have simply been impossible to survive.

We were told to again board a paddle-wheeler ferry at the dock, and sail to Wedel, a village further downstream. We each had a small bundle to carry, all that remained of our worldly possessions. My violin, a briefcase, and a bundle of bedding were in my charge. A caravan of trucks stood near the Elbe ferry station. Papa deposited us on a bench that was used for the limited service, now nonexistent. He walked over to the row of vehicles standing nearby, chatted with a few of the men who were to drive the trucks, and realized that the *Ausgebombten* were to be scattered throughout Holstein province. One of the drivers was a farmer named Holm. He asked if my father had ever worked on a farm.

"I worked as a ranch hand in Texas when I first entered the United States," he told him, because a few moments later, we handed our baggage to farmer Holm.

The vehicle bounced along the cobblestone road with us crammed in between our belongings, away from the familiar site of the Elbe, to the inland chaussee which led to the hamlet of Holm. The farmer and the town with the same name, we wondered? We now drove through remote fields of feed corn, meadows sprinkled with two tone Holstein cows, and stopped at an ancient thatch roofed farm house. The design of the North German *Strohdach Bauernhof* was typical of that countryside. Frau Holm ushered us into *das Altenteil*, the living and bedroom section reserved for the retired, or elder, generation.

That first evening, we all ate together in the large kitchen. Herr and Frau Holm, Anna, the Ukranian maid, and Serge, the Polish farmhand made us feel welcome. Papa had pledged to help bring in the harvest with the two men. Mama and Frau Holm canned vegetables, and simmered large vats of sweet smelling jams as well as preserves. My sister Erika and I attached ourselves to Anna, who was a fiery buckboard driver. She snapped her whip around the choicest bright apples, letting them plop into our skirted laps as we raced through the orchard. We plucked greens for the rabbits, gathered the eggs in the chicken coop, helped clean the hutch, and feed the chickens. Anna tried to teach me how to milk a cow, but

I was swatted by a tail when my cold fingers startled Lora, Anna's favorite cow.

"How did you learn to milk cows?" I asked Anna. She laughed, and in her broken German, she replied, "*Auf mein Papa's Hof! Ich komm' von Ukraine, viele Morgen Land.*" She had been taken from her parent's large estate by the German occupation forces in Russia. We conversed with hands and feet, gesturing when her German vocabulary was exhausted. I tried in English, then in the few French words I knew, to no avail. She asked if I had been born in Hamburg, and I explained that I came from New York. She touched her heart when we spoke of our homes, and started to cry. "When the war is over, we will all go home," she said with great conviction. I, however, was rather dubious even of the chances for our very survival, and did not reply.

On Sunday, Anna donned her native Ukranian costume. She had just finished embroidering the elaborate designs of the sleeves and bodice of the blouse. I admired her skill in handicrafts as well as her expertise with the animals. As a city girl, my labor contribution was strictly supportive with menial tasks. Papa rode in huge stacks of hay, stored them in the loft, and raced out again into the fields to get all the harvest in before the summer rainstorms hit.

The cock announced the start of another day. The old dog squeezed through the door into our rooms each morning when Anna brought us our breakfast. She opened our living quarters with all the courtliness of a Zarina's lady's maid, balancing the large tray like an expert juggler. Our belongings, topped by my violin, were heaped in a corner like some forgotten past. We adapted to our host's household as if we had no other occupation or plan. Again, the deep vibration of hundreds of motors flying overhead woke us. Papa stepped out into the *Diele*. Farmer Holm urged us to take shelter in the cow barn. We obliged him only not to hurt his feelings, for we knew the ten meters of hay in the loft would offer little protection to a direct bomb strike. Serge crouched next to the bull, who was kept on the far end of the stable. Periodically, the huge animal would chomp at his chain, stomp loudly, huff and expel large breaths of air from either fear or the annoyance of an interrupted routine. Anna sat next to her favorite milking cow, gently patting her when the ground shook from a nearby explosion.

"We are in a very safe shelter," farmer Holm joked, his arms folded across his chest, more to assure himself than to convince us. Again the light flickered, followed by an earsplitting thump. The taurus nearly pulled the chain out of the eye bolt in the wall. Serge kicked him to distract him. Frau Holm had covered her ears, and stared into her apron. Papa was chewing on a wisp of hay, the borrowed straw hat tilted to the back of his head, and looked like a Texas rancher. Mama pushed her glasses back up the bridge of her nose, exclaiming, "*Wieder mal Glück gehabt!*" Indeed, we had been lucky once again.

The next morning, Papa and farmer Holm discovered a large bomb crater in one of the meadows, and two heifers were missing. Bits of bloody flesh were stuck to bushes and the fence post. That afternoon, the *Bürgermeister* rode by the farm, holding a piece of paper with Papa's name on it. He was to report to work at the submarine base immediately.

We were constantly aware of, and amazed at the local block warden's and town official's cooperation with the disrupted Hamburg bureaucracy. We had the disconcerting knowledge that we were never out of the reach of the regime. Papa was needed for the repairs to the submarines. By the spring of 1943, the Germans had as many as 235 U-boats in action, and they were considered to be one of the most essential weapons in the arsenal of the Third Reich. The bombed out victims were again to be bumped further inland on a cattle train tomorrow, the Mayor of the tiny hamlet proclaimed. He volunteered to notify the Howaldt Shipyard that we would be on the train with Papa until we found another place to stay.

We gathered for a supper of buttermilk soup, *Bratkartoffeln*, and special farm smoked ham in the large country kitchen. I heard Herr Holm, who was sitting next to my father say, "A toast to you and your family, and lots of luck." Anna leaned over to me, and dropped a package of tattered tissues into my lap. I took my time opening it. Inside the folds of the paper I found a most beautiful pair of blue lace gloves. I uttered my *Danke schön*, and ate the last meal with this kindly family wearing the hand coverings. Anna burst with pride, and I entertained all with mimicry of a grand dame. For dessert, we had some of the delicious compot Mama had helped to process.

In the morning, we collected our gear that had stood forlorn in the corner of our quarters. Farmer Holm had the buckboard ready, and hoisted us and our belongings aboard like pioneers off to another unknown land. Frau Holm had packed some sandwiches for our journey to who knew where? Even had the Holms wanted us to stay, permission had to be granted by the local *Gauleiter*, who was not inclined to be cooperative. The amount of paperwork that every person in Germany generated kept an army of government bureaucrats continually at work. Even the destruction of the city of Hamburg did not prevent the various municipal hierarchies in the surrounding suburbs from wielding their power like little caesars. The higher up party members, of course, were the ones with the most influence., and had control over the district educators, mayors, tax collectors, *Ausweis* and ration card departments. The press had already not been free for several years, so whatever news we received was brought out by the propaganda machine of the National Socialist party. Too many people were now homeless due to the continued bombings by the Allied forces. Each household having an extra room or apartment was required to take in victims of the bombings. My father's *Ausweis* restricted him to the Hamburg city limits. He was a vital but indentured worker on the submarine base, much needed to repair the U-boats that limped into the Neuhof Marine Arsenal after attacking British convoys in the North Atlantic. Rear Admiral Karl Dönitz was the commander of the German submarine fleet who devised the tactics for attacking Allied shipping.

After a short ride in the buckboard, we arrived at a local railway whistle stop to join hundreds of other bombed out victims waiting to board the train to be relocated.

Reichenbach im Traumland

A cattle train pulled up to our area, slowed down, and stopped with screeching brakes. We were given no information about what our destination was to be. "Get them loaded as fast as possible," we overheard the distraught official say to a few volunteers posted along the track. Papa sprang aboard first, then took the baggage which we handed him. We then scrambled laboriously aboard and staked out an area near the sliding door. The box cars quickly filled with the bewildered crowd. Each person crouched, sat, or propped themselves up with their now only belongings. I was hot, and we were sweaty and thirsty. I lay in a grim daze. "*Abfahren!*" was shouted, and the train slowly began to move. Papa leaned out of the still open door to get a last glimpse of farmer Holm, and then partially closed the sliding door, upon the request of some of the women. The strong breeze had begun to whip our hair, causing my ear, made sensitive by my earlier mastoid operations, to ache. I asked my mother if we had a scarf or cap among our belongings. She fished out a kerchief from one of the bags. I was delighted to have it, and tied it in a babushka around my head. The train continued rolling at an erratic pace, sometimes at a mere crawl, other times speeding, then stopping in a remote agricultural area or a forest. A few times, it halted in stations where groups of volunteer women offered us coolaid flavored water, which we greedily drank. The direction of the train frequently changed, the locomotive sometimes pulling, and other times pushing us. Papa and I vainly tried to guess our destination, until we spotted the sign *Wittenberg*. I thought of Martin Luther, who had led the protestant reformation in Germany. I craned my neck out of the door, trying to catch a glimpse of the church or university of the city where Luther had preached and lectured. I had learned that Martin Luther had received the degree of Doctor of Divinity here in 1512. His lecture courses on the Bible brought him much fame as a teacher. Many of his colleagues, and most of his students, supported his struggles with the Roman Catholic church. It was in Wittenberg where Luther had burned the Papal Bull, the burning of which had been part of the cause of his excommunication.

Shortly afterwards, we were rerouted to Magdeburg, where we were unloaded, and dispersed to various homes for several days. We then were regathered to board another train to continue our seemingly aimless shuttling. We began to see signs indicating our nearness to Berlin. The bombardment of that city by allied planes caused us to deviate to the southeast. We were hungry, thirsty, our bones ached, and we were becoming more and more despondent. Papa made the decision to leave the cattle train at the next convenient slowdown. Outside of the lovely town of Reichenbach, surrounded by soft hills, we slid off into the evening twilight. We trudged along the tracks, scurried into the *Bahnhof,* pretending to have arrived on a scheduled passenger train. Papa went to the *Auskunft.* A woman in the information booth sat daydreaming. "Where do I find an official to get lodgings for my family?" Papa asked. She sprang to life behind the counter, and asked for my father's *Ausweis.* She was at a loss when she read the notation "Not to leave the limits of *Gross Hamburg.*" An elderly policeman was summoned, who escorted us to a nearby *Polizeistation.* My mother, sister Erika, and I were deposited on a bench, surrounded by our belongings. Papa was taken into an office. After a while, Mama asked where the toilets were. We also asked the desk sergeant to watch our bundles while we washed as best as we could. Soon Papa emerged from the office triumphantly waving a document. We each grabbed our luggage, and hurried out of the police station.

"*Ich habe die nötigen Papiere!*" he whispered to my mother. Necessary papers in hand, Erika and I schlepped after our parents. It turned out to be quite a walk from the center of town, but we were still able to enjoy the evening breeze through picturesque Reichenbach. Our destination was *Schlachthofstrasse*, a wide fairway with just a few houses along a hillside. On one side, we passed an industrial building housing a slaughter house next to a sausage factory. We continued climbing until we arrived at a grand looking apartment house with garages and a stable in the rear. Across the road were meadows and orchards, which seemed to be part of this complex. Now Papa took out the document he had slipped into his jacket pocket.

"We are looking for number 39," he proclaimed. He further examined the paper and read the black stamp at the bottom. "*Zwangseinquartierung!*" he solemnly said. "What does that mean, Papa?" I asked.

"It means that these people are being forced to take us in. We shall just stay for the night, and leave as soon as possible." He rang the doorbell at the gate. While what seemed to be hours, I wondered what the opposite of faith was. My mother's face gave me the answer. Despair was in her eyes, and she had already turned away from the entrance, when the large door opened. I was exhausted, ready to burst into tears, but managed a slight smile, when a middleaged, dark haired woman met my eyes. She looked at all of us questioningly, "*Ausgebombte?*" We nodded. "*Herzlich Willkommen! Wir warten schon lange, kommt 'rein!*" We looked at each other in surprise. Papa then handed her the document from the police station. Frau Schneider then saw the official stamp next to her name. "That's not right," she proclaimed emphatically, ushering us into the corridor. "My parents built this apartment house, and they are the owners of the slaughterhouse and sausage factory, as well as most of the property on this hill. They now live on the first floor, my brother and his family on the second landing, and my husband and I are on the third *Etage*." She called into the hall that visitors had come, and would they please come and help carry their belongings to the room prepared for them. Doors from each landing were thrown open, footsteps scurried on the terra cotta landings and marble steps. We were led into a large room on the third floor with a single bed on each right and left far wall. A picture window with custom made lace curtains and drapes over them separated the beds. Near the entrance stood a table with four chairs, and an overhead lamp. An immense chiffonier with shelves, drawers, and hanging closet space was waiting for our possessions.

"The bathroom is across the hall. I will turn on the hot water for your baths," Frau Schneider called out cheerfully. "Tomorrow, we will go into the *Waschküche* to help clean your clothes." While we luxuriated one by one in the bath, Frau Schneider busied herself in the kitchen. Papa, who was the last out of the bath, taking the least amount of time, had pulled a sport shirt out of his valise. I recognized it from our New York City days. Mama was already organizing the clothes we had in our bags, suitcases, and bundles. Frau Schneider tapped on the door with her foot, as she was carrying a large tray with a soup tureen, plates, spoons, and a bowl of fruit. We were surprised as well as delighted.

AFTER A WONDERFUL night's sleep with no interruptions of alarm sirens, Erika and I awoke. Papa and Mama were still sleeping in the other twin bed. We whispered to each other, but they soon heard us. Papa's first words were that he would have to return to the police station in Reichenbach to get a train pass for Hamburg. "I will get in terrible trouble with the regime if I do not report for work at the Neuhof submarine base," he said to my mother.

Mama packed whatever clothes were my father's, but persuaded him to wait at least another day until she had washed and dried the grimy garments that he had been wearing since leaving Holm. He agreed reluctantly, however, under the condition that he would bring me to a local school first before heading to the local police station. Frau Schneider knocked on our door to invite us to breakfast in her kitchen. We appreciated the gesture of her opening her home to us so freely. However, Papa brought up the subject of the stamp on our papers again. I remember him saying that we did not want to be a hardship for her by taking up a room that might otherwise be needed by her family. "Please stay," she pleaded with us. "I believe the *Gauleiter* has a grudge against us. The local authorities are jealous of our family possessions and land wealth. They have tried on several occasions to take over our properties." My parents understood those tactics only too well. The bureaucrats connected to the regime were hostile to us as well, however, the Hamburg officials often hid behind the old Hanseatic League laws in our favor, much to the chagrin of the Nazis.

I WAS BROUGHT to the *Albert Schule*. The principal of the school had a spacious office. He sat behind a huge oak desk with a large portrait of the *Führer* on the wall above him. He appeared to be annoyed upon hearing my father's northern German accent, eyeing us suspiciously. When he heard that we were bombed out victims, his secretary was called. I looked at my father admiringly. He stood dressed in his Manhattan tailored dark blue jacket, his favorite nautical attire, which he had saved from the allied bombing devastation. My dress, also, Papa had snatched from my closet before the flames had consumed our apartment house and the entire neighborhood.

The efficient, well dressed secretary entered. She motioned for my father to sit across the room on a chair near her small desk. She then asked me which grade I was in. "Well, I just competed to be accepted in the Hamburg Oberbau." That answer in turn annoyed her. Papa and I looked at each other and grinned.

"What is your name?" she asked my father. "Please show me your *Ausweis*," Upon examining the document, she asked for the Reichenbach police residence permit, but said nothing about the Gross Hamburg restriction. I was then asked to fill out a short questionnaire. My New York birthplace and spelling of my name raised some questions. The Nazi uniformed principal was buried behind a newspaper, but listened, and peeked out every few minutes. The secretary then took me to a classroom headed by a bedraggled, sour faced, bearded, ramrod of a teacher. I was assigned a seat. In the meantime, my father went from the Albert

Schule to the police station. He gave the authorities notice of our wonderful lodgings in a most hospitable house. He mentioned how pleased he was for the courtesy shown him by the Reichenbach police. "Please let me know by which route my Hamburg employers want me to return." He later related the event to us when we gathered for supper.

I SAT FIDGETING among the 35 students, but persuaded myself to just listen motionlessly. The phenomenon of language is a most remarkable feature of every culture. For years, I was unaware of the fact that, as a young child, I had been conversing and thinking in both English and German. I also felt that I had a different personality within myself in each of these cultures. I now closed out all distractions. In my trance-like pose, it was apparent to me that I shut out all audible traces of the teacher. How long I remained in that state, I do not know, but suddenly the, to me, disagreeable pedagogue stood threateningly before me. "*Nun, gnädiges Fräulein?*" he inquired. Startled, I looked up. I answered that I was only used to high German, and that I had difficulty understanding his dialect. Well, that statement set off such a verbal barrage upon me, that I removed myself further into my cocoon.

Practically sleepwalking, I arrived at 39 *Schlachthofstrasse* after Frau Schneider happened to meet me at the gate. She led me up the stairs into her beautiful sitting room containing a piano and an entire wall of shelves of books. She invited me to use the room as often as I wanted. Her library was a great comfort to me, and contributed much to expanding my horizons. I remember the book by Dr. L.L. Zamenhof, the creator of the international language Esperanto. He had signed his 1887 work, D-ro Esperanto, which meant "one who hopes." He believed that the entire world could be relieved of much of its savagery in two ways. "Every land belongs morally and materially to its sons (and I hoped that he meant its daughters as well), on a basis of completely equal rights." To help bring this about, it would be necessary to call the countries by neutral geographical names, instead of by the names of races. In a kingdom called Russia, the Russians believe themselves to be the possessors, and the Letts, Estonians, and Poles were oppressed. In a land called Poland, the Poles feel themselves to be masters, while Jews, Ruthenians, and Lithuanians bewailed their humiliation. "Most Serene Republics," the different races had considered themselves on more equal terms merely on account of the name. Similarly, the words "Swiss Confederation," "United States of America," "Brazil," give no particular race the right to look upon the country as its exclusive own, and other inhabitants as tolerated foreigners. "Esperanto should be the second language all students all over the world should learn, in order to be able to communicate with each other." How wonderful, I thought. When this war is over, and I get back to New York City, that would be a most worthwhile cause to look into.

PAPA'S CLOTHES WERE washed. Mama had packed one of the valises with all that he still owned. The train would take him to Hamburg, and he would write us upon his arrival, after reporting to the Howaldt shipyard.

WE, THAT IS, my mother, six year junior sister Erika, and I became part of the family complex of the *Schlacthofstrasse*. Frau Schneider, who did not have any children of her own, introduced me to her handsome nephew Wolfgang. He was a few years older than I, and a student in the *Gymnasium*. He was a very cheerful lad with a beautiful singing voice, who broke out into song upon entering the hallway. His tenor voice rose up from the parterre through to the four flights of the *Treppenhaus* with the magnificent acoustics of an opera house. He had either seen or been told by his aunt about my violin, for he tried to persuade me to play. However, I could not bear the mention of my fiddle without being reminded of my music teacher Herr Pahl, his wife, and my friend Elfriede and her family. The cruel memories of the horrific air raid attacks culminating in the hellish fire storms arose before me once again. I believed my friends to have perished. I shook and cried uncontrollably. Wolfgang was startled, but each day continued his serenade of *Glühwürmchen, Glühwürmchen glimmere, glimmer*, announcing himself to me and his family upon entering the marble hall of the apartment house.

Automatically, I fell into a routine, sleepwalking to the Albert *Schule*. When there, I had no recollection of having received any kind of useful communication. However, I felt that Frau Schneider tried to guide me. She first introduced me to the books in her library, but then, when she saw that I had buried myself in mountains of literature, I was invited to see her miniature mountain goats. She had several of them, little, dark brown, almost black kids, erratically spring-bucking through the fresh smelling hay in the backyard barn next to a large garage complex. The garage housed Herr Schneider's business. The stable also housed a few horses, one of which I believe belonged to Wolfgang.

Besides the tiny Toggenburg goats, or perhaps they were descendants of the wild Persian goats of southwestern Asia, she also kept some white ones. These were from 100 to 120 pounds when fully grown. Like the cow, the goat belongs to the cattle family. It, too, is a grass eater. It has a special stomach that permits it to hastily swallow its food, store the grass, and then regurgitate to chew it later as a cud. They do not grow as large as sheep, also do not herd easily, but have an individualized personality. So I found out, when Frau Schneider gave me the task of escort to bring some half dozen goats across the road to the meadow beyond the fruit orchards. To my consternation, I found them anything but cooperative.

"Take any book along from my library, Helen," she called out cheerfully. "Just see that the goats stay in the meadow, and watch out that they don't eat any of the fruit." There are three chief classes of goats. The first are the Swiss goats, which have pointed ears. These are the most important ancestors of most American and European breeds. The second type is the Nubian with drooping ears. The third type is the group that grows wool. Frau Schneider had the most obstinate of goats, like the old Germans that emigrated to North America, especially from my family. The first day, I took on the task of goat herder alone, but under the tutelage of Frau Schneider. She had given me a cane to lead them across the road, and then along the path as we skirted the fruit orchards. I opened the gate into the sloping meadow, held it, and listened to the goats bleating joyously. They leaped, pronked, ran, and experienced the sheer freedom of the moment. I laughed at their exuberance. What a sight!

The following day, after another trance-like ordeal into the Albert *Schule*, I asked my mother if Erika could come with me to help with the goats. Out of Frau Schneider's library, I had already started reading Havelock Ellis' book *The Dance of Life*. I was anxious to continue, since some of his other works were already familiar to me. All day during class, I thought about the joy of dance. The Nazi regime had *Tanz Verbot*. I recalled how my Hamburg friend Irmgard had always chided me for singing and dancing to American tunes. The most recent hit song I remembered from New York was:

The merry-go-round broke down,
as we went round and round-
The lights went low,
We both said, Oh!
As the merry-go-round went oompah, oompah, oompah pah
   pah.

"Das ist verboten, Helen!" Irmgard would admonish me. My father told me that *Swingcliquen* had been arrested. Humming or singing American jazz was forbidden. Louis Armstrong, Ted Stauffer, or Benny Goodman were musicians in conflict with the New Order.

Havelock Ellis mentions, in the chapter on the art of dancing, "Indeed a dance still lingers always at the heart of music and even the heart of the composer. Mozart, who was himself an accomplished dancer, used often to say, so his wife stated, that it was dancing, not music, that he really cared for."

In my New York elementary social studies book about the American Indian, their culture fascinated me. War dances were the first I tried to imitate. But, as far as music was concerned, Indian music was to me very much a Johnny-one-note. The American Indian, to my ear, did not have pretty music. The study of herbs, which my grandmother, the Prussian good witch of the north relative, knew so much about, encouraged my rain dance routine during drought. "It does not hurt to get the ears and eyes of the Almighty by any means," she had a habit of saying.

The book, *The Dance of Life*, was for me an epiphany, a manifestation, an essential nature or meaning of something, an intuitive grasp of reality, an illuminating discovery. Dance is the earliest form of expression in any society. From the dawn of civilization it was the joy of life, but more so, it banished frustrations of weather, war, and sorrow, which helped bring relief of pain. So it was for me. Each day, Erika and I would guide our goats to the lush meadow. We picked wild flowers, made wreaths for our hair, and danced the women's dances of ancient times. Imaginary dances of the northern goddesses, or the mother countries of all civilized dancing, Egyptian, Greek temple dances, and Tunisian hair dances. We improvised to jazz, waltzes, tangos, polkas, swing, and folk tunes, beating on sticks, or humming whatever melodies popped into our heads. We stomped, hopped, skipped, and jumped across the sunlit terrain. We whirled, twirled, turned, shook, and collapsed with exhaustion into quivering heaps. The pygmy goats looked on in wonderment, but then they joined in, too, bleating when we stopped to laugh.

The middle East gave full importance to song and dance, I remember reading. The ancient Semitic shepherds had their shepherd dances. So it became our task by tending our flock of goats, we would make up dances. We pretended to be Arab dancers, using our canes as swords, or twisted and turned to imitate the movements of the planets. We became mesmerized Dervishes, gesture dancers of Hawaii or India. We dipped and swayed, forgetting for the moment that the war was still raging on.

However, Havelock Ellis says that the ecstatic Hindu dance in honor of the pre-Aryan hill god, afterwards Shiva, became in time a great symbol, the clearest image of the activity of God. The dance thus becomes the presentation of a divine drama, the vital reenactment of a sacred history. In this way, ritual arises. The divine services of the American Indian took the form of "Set dances", each with its own name, song, steps, and costumes.

At this point, the early Christian, worshiping the divine body, was able to join in spiritual communication with the ancient Egyptian, or later, Japanese, or the modern American Indian. What some consider the earliest Christian ritual, the "Hymn of Jesus", assigned to the second century is nothing more than a sacred dance.

PAPA WROTE A letter from Hamburg, at least that is what it was postmarked, but we knew that he was actually working day and night at the Neuhof submarine base repairing U-boats. We had not been quite clear as to where he managed to sleep, eat, or store his one valise of clothes. Our previous mementoes of all of our family life in New York had been burned in the terrible Allied bombing raids of the city. *Gomorrah* had brought death to over 60,000 people. How thankful we were to have survived that destruction. Our entire neighborhood was nothing more than a still smoldering pile of rubble, even now, Papa reported. "The entire *Lahrmannstrasse* is gone. The city is a dismal, grey place." He was working long hours in the submarine bunker, never knowing if it was day or night. Only when the giant doors or the pool gates were opened could he see daylight. Sometimes he just slept underneath the cranes or heavy lifting equipment for an hour or two, then went back to the U-boat repairs.

"The crew members have barracks on the roof of the bunker, while we ready their vessels for another sortie into the Atlantic. Then, some more of the thousands of the Allied planes try to knock down the heavy Flak on each corner of the bunker roofs. I have learned to rest whenever there is a lull in the war zone."

We had suffered no air raids in bucolic Reichenbach. While tending my flock of goats, I would daydream of America. During this period, we did not know of the fate of my father's brother Hans, who we later learned had been interned with an American born Japanese physician in a Hartford, CT detention center. Only this past year have I come across the book *Undue Process–The Untold Story of America's German Alien Internees*, by Arnold Krammer. It reveals a startling fact. American history has overlooked the injustice perpetrated against the German population of the USA. The American government ordered the arrests and internment of thousands of German aliens, including women and children, in federal prison camps without trial or the opportunity for appeal. Only recently released government documents and never before published photographs give a disturbing, eye opening look at one of this country's best kept secrets of WWII.

WE HAD ANOTHER great distraction in the Schneider household. It was *Mirtzel*, a young mop-like dog. He was to be trained for hunting, Wolfgang volunteered. However, *Mirtzel* looked for all the world like a stuffed toy come to life. He only loved fun and play. The following Sunday, Frau Schneider had the dog on a leash, and we were invited to join them for *Spazierengehen*. We walked on serene, hilly roads, with Erika and I taking turns holding *Mirtzel* on the leash. When we were away from any settlement, Frau Schneider let him roam. The hound no sooner was free, when he suddenly and unexpectedly turned into a hunting animal. He ran across a wide field with an old farmhouse and barn at the end of it. No amount of calling or coaxing by Frau Schneider could stop the dog. All of us dashed after him. *Mirtzel* vanished into the barn, which immediately exploded into a pandemonium of wild cackling. He emerged holding a chicken in his jaws, proudly prancing towards us, and dropped the fowl at our feet. Erika picked up the dead chicken, scooping it into her apron. Frau Schneider yoohooed for the farmers. "They are probably having a nap." Since noone came out to us, she left some money on a window sill, weighing it down with a stone.

When we got home, Mama prepared the chicken for our consumption by immersing it in hot water prior to plucking its feathers. Frau Schneider gave her fresh vegetables from her garden, and we had wonderful chicken soup for several days.

Mama had corresponded with her aunt Guste, who invited us to share their attic rooms in their retirement home in *Halstenbeck*. She thought that it would be better for us to be closer to where my father was, although we felt welcome and comfortable where we now were. The next morning, when I went to the school, I asked the teacher for an attendance report for the time I had been present in his class. He flatly and unreasonably refused to provide me with any kind of verification. I promptly left the classroom and burst into the principal's office. *Rector* Schlag sat behind his huge, opulent oak desk in his brown uniform. The hypnotic eyes of the *Führer* followed my every move as I stared at the portrait behind the principal. I called out a loud, clear: "Heil Hitler!" I raise my arm in the proper stance, and to my amazement, he jumped up to greet me likewise. For an instant I hesitated, but then I asked for my reference. He looked at me in surprise. "Your teacher is the one to ask for a class document," he called out. I brazenly replied, "You know who I am." He inquired what my name was, and without bothering to check the spelling, signed his name, and filled in *"Führung und Haltung gut"*, added the eagle with swastika seal with a loud thud. *"Danke schön kein Aufwiedersehen!"* I called out mischievously.

Return to Hamburg; Saving the Children

We returned to Hamburg perched on our assorted baggage, in the long narrow walkway of an overcrowded passenger train. Our fellow travelers were mostly military personnel, or displaced victims like us. Nobody traveled for pleasure. We arrived in the midst of another air raid, and took shelter in some underground tunnel near the *Hauptbahnhof*. We emerged after the all clear to get our connection to a local train to Elmshorn, the last stop on that track. We detrained at Halstenbeck, and walked several miles to intrude into the tranquil household of Onkel Ernst and Tante Guste. After attending the local school for a time, I was shipped to my beloved summer retreat in the heath country surrounding the towns of Buchholz and Jesteburg. Now it was late into autumn. The Oberbau was the school I should have attended. The Weihe Children's Home had been converted to cram more occupants into the former vacation retreat than was originally intended. We slept in tight dormitory quarters. The age group was from five to fifteen. Several of the children had lost their fathers on the fighting fronts, and their mothers during the bombings as well. Boys and girls were separated by lining up lockers into the center of the room. This arrangement was necessary due to the need of heating the dorm with a tiled wood and coal burning stove. The other large room had been divided in similar fashion for our adult caretakers. Since none of the smaller rooms could be heated, they left them empty after September. Schwester Lina was in charge, and Frau Rothmann organized the kitchen facilities. I was recruited as an additional instructor for the five to twelve year olds, and made *Stubenälteste* to all the girls after lightsout. My height gave me the authority that I did not have in years of age, but aroused resentment in the older girls. The library was open to me at all hours, which I needed for the planning of my lessons, since I was also training myself to teach. The trips to the reading room were envied by all, even though they did not read as much as I.

On one of my previous vacation visits, after one of my violin practice sessions in the forest, I was attacked by several fellow campers whom I had thought to be my friends. When they came charging at me, I at first believed that it was because they could not stand my repetitious etudes. I was tied to a tree, and chants of *Amerikanerin!* hissed from their lips. I realized that they had listened to a recent broadcast of a speech by Adolf Hitler. The *Führer* had incensed them with his passionate propaganda and hate campaign against the enemy of the Reich. They had been inflamed by his rhetoric, and had found in me an outlet for their frustrations. The sudden appearance of one of the counselors saved me from further abuse. The hurt of this appalling deed by boys and girls whom I had trusted stayed with me for a very long time. I did not mention the incident to any of the other counselors, but thereafter became watchful and leery of provoking my peers.

Schwester Lina gave me further responsibilities with extra, envied privileges. The other children did not know that I was putting in hours working in the kitchen, and the neighboring farmers' potato fields, while they enjoyed their afternoon naps. In order not to have petty jealousies further mar my existence, I started telling Hollywood and gangster stories every evening at bedtime. I connected my tales with cowboys and Indians, making two or three of my dormitory dwellers the heroes of the nightly episodes. Like Scheherazade, I spun my tales to be continued, and to be left in peace for the rest of the day. The stories became regular entertainment, and I was bribed with desserts, flowers, and trinkets if I included them to be the heroes or heroines for the nightly sequels. The grownups took to standing behind the door to listen in to members of the incongruous mixture of Chicago gangsters and cowboys riding across the plains of the Dakotas, being chased by Sioux Indians, who had adopted Günther or Werner to come along on the raids. They sat in the teepee with Geronimo, smoking the peace pipe. The gangsters were pursued by war-whooping Redskins into California territory. Al Capone raced to Hollywood, disguised at MGM studios as George Raft's sidekick. The earth trembled, swallowing the bad men while the brave Indians stood on the jagged mountain edges, silhouetted against the orange sunset of the Arizona sky. The Lone Ranger and Tonto would leap across the crevasse waving hello to my heroes, inviting them to a feast of roasted buffalo, Indian pudding, and mountains of popcorn washed down with toasts of root beer firewater. My villains never died, noone for that matter, always reappearing in other chapters, or the following day in the Carlsbad Caverns, terrified by bats and Count Dracula of Mexilvania.

Christmas of 1943 was spent at the *Weihe Kinderheim.* Herr Rothmann got dressed as Santa Claus, and we each received an apple and some cookies. After each of us either recited a poem, played an instrument, or sang some Christmas songs in front of the decorated Tannenbaum, we were each given a small package. I was happy to receive a bar of perfumed soap wrapped in a pink wash cloth, a tooth brush, and some tooth paste. The soap we could normally purchase with our ration cards consisted of a grey pumace gritty mass, which I was terribly allergic to. How I delighted in touching and sniffing the beautiful white prewar soap! It was a hard bar, and I carefully let it dry out after each use, then stored it in a special metal soap box that my mother had given me along.

In January of the new year, my mother wrote that Papa had found us another place to live in Hamburg again. An old, historical merchant's house on the *Deichstrasse,* across the canal from piles of rubble. The ancient empty building was under historical conservation, and was *baufällig.* "It could collapse any day," the city building inspector had warned, while the museum staff photographed the ornamental plaster ceilings. Notwithstanding this threat, we quickly decided to move in. Papa slung a temporary electric power line through the window to his friend Karson's apartment several houses away. Papa had done his own construction test, and was convinced that the structure would survive our stay, and so it has. To this day, I still see postcards with pictures of this row of houses identified as *Alte Häuser am Nicolaifleet*. When we moved into the two rooms facing the canal, the seagulls entertained us with their aerial antics outside the window. The cases of empty bottles stored in the basement clanked and thumped us to sleep, or alternately startled us awake with the changing of the tide as the water filled the lower floor. Hamburg has often been called "The Venice of the North", and we were certainly aware of that appellation while living in this location. The alley cats roaming this area were the size of diminutive tigers. Bold fighters they were, with chewed off ears, fiery red gashes of unhealed wounds, bobbed tails, and crooked smiles. We often saw them dragging rats still twitching with life. The tomcat would snarl, and the rat would get in a last bite, further distorting the feline's grimace. Water was trucked into the neighborhood twice a week, and we never had enough containers for our supply. The wagon came while I was in school, and Mama did all the heavy lugging. Papa was unexpectedly drafted into the army, to be sent to Holland for training. I had abandoned my comforting memories of my Manhattan island, thinking of my eventual return only with discouragement and indifference. The dreary, destroyed sections of the city added to the depression. People lived in makeshift holes of former basements among the rubble. Curls of smoke would be visible over mounds of bricks and ashes. Hovels housed entire families in subterranean caves. We felt lucky to have a roof over our heads. I tried to cheer myself in my worst hours by visiting the Hamburg Museum, which by some miracle was still intact. I admired the craftsmanship of the armor exhibited in the *Rittersaal*, while yet realizing the futility of hope for peace. The only solace I found was in walks to the harbor, and my now chronic despair became refreshed with the vitality of the river's movements. It did not matter if I was embraced by fog constricting my vision of the Elbe, just knowing it was there was enough. Did the water really extend to another continent, or was it all merely a childhood fantasy?

Feudalism Still Lives

The meager rations, primitive living conditions, and sporadic air attacks contributed to a lethargic academic record in many students. Educators were aware of this, and transports of children had been organized into groups for several years already. Before we had been bombed out, and while I still was attending elementary *Volkschule*, several neighborhood children had been sent to various country communities to be taught in less war disturbed areas. They would be away from the parental influence for months, or even years at a time, coming home for brief emergencies, holiday visits only, or not at all. Inge, one of the girls I had known from the old neighborhood, as we now referred to our lost property, had the speech pattern of a Bavarian; others adopted the Hessian or Saxon inflections, depending on the regions the children were sent to. My teachers and principal of the Hamburg *Oberbau* now collected groups of 25 girls to be sent out of the city. What a wonderful surprise it was to find Elfriede standing in line to fill out the required paperwork. We had been told about the registration announcement on the radio by Frau Karson, as we no longer had a radio of our own. Her daughter Ursula was also one of the girls to be educated outside of the city. I had the option of two destinations, but decided on a transport with Elfriede to the *Prignitz*. In the tiny hamlet of Frehne, we were distributed from the one room schoolhouse to the local households that had beds to spare. Since most of the men from their teens to over half a century were on one of the occupation or fighting fronts, an empty berth was available in almost every house. Our teacher, Herr Walter Rosenbaum, was lodged in the apartment adjacent to the school house. His wife had become the instructor for the local children, who, before our arrival, had to walk several kilometers to school in Meyenburg. The arrival of the *"Hamburger Mädel"*, as we became known, was a major event in this agricultural community. The aloof Countess, still the figurehead in the ancient feudal system, welcomed us. The almost senile *Bürgermeister* introduced us to the locally assigned Berlin Nazi party leaders. We were greeted with several renditions of *Volkslieder* by the population. A woman wearing a red fox fur hat grabbed my hand and suitcase simultaneously. I was housed in the *Försterei*, the local forest ranger's home. The first morning in my new surroundings, I was awakened by odd sounds of scraping. My hostess, the ranger's wife, like most of the households without men, had taken over her husband's tasks. The hide of a fox had been pulled over an ironing board, and she was removing the flesh. She had already milked the two cows, stirred the fire in the hearth to heat the *Ersatzkaffee* and wash water. Her daughter Waltraut, a few years younger than I, opened her eyes in the bed next to me about the same time as I. My *"Guten Morgen"* remained like sky writing in the chilly morning air. My exposed nose felt frozen as I jumped out of the warm and cozy feather bed, and dressed briskly to hurry into the heated *Diele*. Every winter evening, a hot brick, or warm water bottle would be placed into our beds, otherwise it would have been difficult to warm up sufficiently to fall asleep. On the last day of the January thaw, we, as well as the weather, had melted into an easier pattern of living. It was my birthday, and my foster mother had baked several yeast cakes and fancy fruit torts. She had invited Elfriede and two more of my classmates, Ursula Karson and Marion Meyer. We all had become fast friends. The closed *Gute Stube* was opened for the occasion. We had a chance to inspect the numerous examples of taxidermy. Dozens of beady glass eyes stared at us, while we enjoyed my birthday treats. Bucks, martens, foxes, and weasels frozen in time watched. This overwhelming display of the art of mounting specimens both astounded and dismayed me as an animal lover. The ranger was a skilled hunter who had been employed by the Countess, who owned most of the woodland around the hamlet. The fox hide on the ironing board was afterwards tanned and prepared, and soon was to warm the neck of my hostess when she bicycled to the mansion of her benefactress. The Countess von Gravenitz was gossiped about, and was the live soap opera heroin of the town.

ELFRIEDE LIVED NEXT door to me in the dairy. Marion and Ursula were lodged on prosperous *Bauernhöfe*. In most farm houses, the women were the head of the households, except for a few old grandfathers, who were treated as if they were in charge, however the women really ran the show. On opposite sides of the hamlet, two buildings housed Russian prisoners of war. The babushka-draped women were escorted by one rifle carrying old German guard, disbursed along the main cobble stone road into their designated farms each morning, and brought back to their compound each evening. The Russian men had two gun-carrying guards, a bent, arthritic farmer, and the teenage village idiot. If an escape had ever been planned by the Russians, it could easily have been accomplished. The ploughing, tending, harvesting and farm chores, were all completed by prisoner of war laborers, many from rural areas of the Ukraine. In one of the households of my classmates, a woman from Berlin lodged. She was the head of the Nazi Party of the district, intensely disliked by most of the farm women. She became the protagonist in their daily soap opera of gossip. *"Die schwarze Dame"*, or, *"die Berlinerin"* were her dramatic handles, ours was mostly as a collective *"die Hamburger Mädchen"*. The sound of rapidly galloping horses, followed by the turning wheels of an elegant black carriage, reminded me of stagecoach travel in our old West. *"Die Gräfin"*, the townspeople would whisper, and rush to the road to catch a glimpse of the Countess passing by. Two black horses were currently in the harness, although *"sechs Rappen"* is what she had available before Hitler had confiscated four of her dark steeds for the war effort. Oh, yes, the war was still raging on all fronts, but in this tranquil and remote rural feudal system community the effects of the battles and bombings were a distant shadow of reality. Nothing had changed here in hundreds of years. Our Hamburg teacher taught us the required curriculum, augmented by his many personal hobbies of art, music, language, botany, and philosophy. We were shaped into a quite satisfactory choir. I was part of the alto section, and for holidays, political or other ceremonial occasions, sang or bowed my violin, with Elfriede playing the piano. Händel, Bach, Beethoven, and Brahms selections, Schubert Lieder, and folk tunes our parents and grandparents had sung for generations were our standard choices.

I WALKED IN the beautiful forest that touched the edges of wild flower dotted meadows, that I thought would never bloom. The winter seemed to go on forever, and in the spring, the rains turned the soil to a muddy morass. My only pair of leather shoes were in sorry shape, and my foster mother gave me a pair of wooden clogs. The regime had also sent along a Hitler Youth leader to continue our Nazi indoctrination. However, Herr Rosenbaum kept us extremely busy with lots of homework carefully calculated to undermine the political influence. He overtly sympathized with the Youth Leader, but diplomatically stressed the importance of an overall education, which he had to instill in all of us. "Do you speak any language other than German?" he would ask the young Party member. Of course, she did not, nor did she have training in music or other liberal arts. "Perhaps you could attend some of the classes, if you wish," he would suggest, "unless you have other duties to perform." She emphasized her prime duty to educate us in the memorial, victory, and other Party services. "Of course," Herr Rosenbaum would solemnly agree. "That is why I am conducting and training the girls to perform in a choir, and Helen and Elfriede will be playing "*ihre Glanzmusikstücke*". He left the Nazi Horst Wessel song, the German national anthem, and the sad war memorial song, "*Ich hat' einen Kameraden*", to the youth leader Hannelore to conduct. He was an accomplished violinist, so I was able to enjoy private lessons, and when he thought my progress to be satisfactory, he would have Elfriede join us whenever we could find a place with a piano.

Elfriede had the best grades in English, which was an embarrassment for me, and spurred me on to spend more time in expanding my own English vocabulary. We also had lessons in French, in which Elfriede again took top honors. Marion seemed to take very naturally to English, later worked for the British occupation forces, and eventually married an RAF pilot.

Hannelore, the BDM (*Bund Deutscher Mädchen*) leader, gifted me with a Hitler Youth uniform, which , although I only had very few other articles of clothes to wear, I disdainfully donned for my farm chores. My job consisted in herding the geese to the meadow for the day, and bringing them back to their stall at night. Hannelore was horrified to see me have so little regard for my Nazi outfit. Smiling sweetly, I placed a farm apron over the blouse and skirt, and tied a floral scarf around my neck.

In the evenings, we would sit around the tables knitting, sewing, or crocheting. I told stories while podding peas, unstringing beans, or changing hair styles with the other girls. While the large, ornately tiled *Kachelofen* was still needed for heat, winter apples snapped and sizzled, filling the room with the delicious aroma of their juices. Summer evenings were like the songs we sang: *Abendfriede über all, nur am Bach die Nachtigal.* One particular beautiful sunset, we sat outside in the tiny flower garden of the local *Gastwirtschaft*. I was again coaxed into telling stories. The local people were so unworldly, that my descriptions of the waterfronts of Hamburg, New York, ships, and the ocean, were to many an entirely new milieu. As I spun my tales, we watched the spectacular colors of the setting sun. A soft breeze ruffled the leaves of the mighty oak we sat under. Men's voices drifted by singing the melancholy Russian tunes of their homeland. I stopped talking in the middle of a sentence, as we listened to the male chorus. The skill and selection of the variety of melodies was so unexpected, that it touched us deeply. Tears streamed down our cheeks, and we spontaneously clapped our hands as if we were in a formal concert hall. After the applause, we caught our collective breaths and reshifted our bodies, when, to our surprise women's voices could be heard. Minor key airs floated across the peaceful village in a nocturnal serenade. Then, as if on cue, the male and female voices blended into a choir from opposite sides of Frehne.

THE WALKS THROUGH the countryside became part of my daily routine. Quite often, I would take my homework and books along, completing my assignments under a tree or in a pasture where my charges spent their summer days. The geese are more comfortable walking on land than swans are. They are smaller, but have longer legs, which are closer to the middle of their bodies. My barnyard friends were proud birds, and it took a while for each of us to adopt to one another. The meadow I escorted them to had a small pond, and they could do much of their own foraging. I never did trust the gander. He pinched me in the calf, and he knew I was frightened of him. The domestic geese are larger than their wild counterparts, and have almost lost all ability to fly.

Returning from the fields one day early in the summer, I saw a lone aircraft drop a parachutist. On my way to the village, several old farmers from the neighboring town came towards me carrying pitchforks. "Did you see a jumper, and notice where he landed?" they asked. I thought it may have been either a British or American reconnaissance plane, and denied having seen it. They then further asked if I had seen any strangers in the area. Herr Rosenbaum had been bird watching some distance away, and I mischievously pointed in his direction. I knew that he could have talked his way out of any precarious situation, but the lone jumper would probably have been hard pressed to explain his presence. The farmers took a while to be convinced, so the gossip from the neighboring *Dorf* central dairy pickup reported. It seems that one of the *Hamburger Mädel* had pointed in Herr Rosenbaum's direction, and his height and unfamiliar garb had created an incident where he had been detained in the local jail until his identity had been confirmed.

A few days later, Elfriede and I put on a concert in the neighboring town. During our absence, my foster mother took my American fountain pen and blue ink bottle, which had been a gift from Averell Harriman to my father, and used it to write a letter to her husband on the Russian front. She had neglected to return them to my drawer, and when I next wrote to my mother, I had to use the standard scratchy quill and black ink from my classroom, which I detested. My mother's return letter demanded to know why I had not used the Parker pen. After several more written exchanges, my mother jumped to the unwarranted conclusion that my foster mother had confiscated it, and wrote an accusing note to her. To this day, I can remember the hurt look on my foster mother's face upon receiving this communication. She took me into the taxidermy display room, and pointed to her husband's desk. There, among the various papers covering the desk, was the pen and ink bottle which she had used and thoughtlessly failed to return.

Life in York

My mother traveled from Hamburg to take me back to the city. The incident with the American fountain pen was too embarrassing for me to remain with the kind foster mother in Frehne. I had discussed it with Herr Rosenbaum, who had agreed that it was an unfortunate situation. He asked me what it was that I wanted to do. The *Oberbau* school system had originally given me two choices of destination. I had chosen to be united with my musical friend Elfriede. I told Herr Rosenbaum how much I had enjoyed our *musizieren* with her, as well as the immense general education I had received from him. I was very sorry to leave him and my other classmates, however, the school board agreed to reassign me. I also thought it for the best in view of the situation.

THE WAR TORN city of Hamburg had not recovered much after the massive July '43 air attacks by the Allied forces. Only the main streets and some of the sidewalks had been cleared, the rubble merely having been piled up higher. Hamburg had no luster, the people no vitality. All looked worn out, tired, depressed, and constantly hungry. City folk have a much harder time surviving during a war than those in the country. The air raids continued without interruption.

Papa had fixed up the apartment in the Deichstrasse as best as the resources of tools, materials, and his limited time with us could afford. For a few weeks, I stayed in the historical house. It was a miserable existence of standing in line for food, coal, and water rations. The nearby charred Nicolai church stood like a haunted tower, its spectral spire pointing ominously to the source of its devastation.

My father had been plucked from his U-boat repair station to be trained as a combat soldier somewhere in Holland. "Papa with his one eye!"Mama lamented, "Totally unsuited for such a training program." I merely shrugged my shoulders in response, to avoid letting out a verbal barrage of frustration. My suppressed feelings of rage were ever present, but I had long learned to control the dam gates from spilling over. We still were not able to acquire a radio again, which I sorely missed, so I would just leave the apartment to take walks.

My paperwork for my new *Oberbau* school destination arrived by mail.   Again, I was to be sent out of Hamburg. This time, I left from my favorite waterfront landmark at *Landungsbrücken*. Most of the harbor and excursion paddle wheelers, steamboats and ferries touching the city, as well as the Gross Hamburg district routes were familiar to me. The metropolitan area of the 1000 year old seaport lay in its 160 square mile center region. The city had been a free state of the German Republic before WWII. More than 60 bridges crossed the canals, and two large (at that time) ones spanned the Elbe. Hamburg was known as the Venice of the north. I now found myself sailing alone to the tiny west bank town of Borstel, my final destination being the town of York. This was meaningful indeed, I thought, since the sound of the town's name was the same as that of my city of birth, New York, although this town actually spelled its name with a J instead of a Y. Leaving the rubble-charred ruins visible from the vessel depressed me further. The ship slid away from the pier. Sadly, I waved to my mother and sister, who stood forlornly at the St. Pauli dock. The familiar St. Michael's church (*der grüne Michel*) stood smudged, but relatively intact, viewing another violent transition of its surroundings. The great stone Bismarck statue stood clutching his mighty sword, his solemn countenance mirroring the desperate times.

I was not inclined to regard the creator of the universe kindly at this time in my life. I did, however, begrudgingly offer thanks for the protection granted our family. Often, I shook my fist at the heavens, lamenting the unfairness at having been transported to Germany at this most unfortuitous time. Then my own mind would offer the logical reason that it had been human folly that had created the circumstances resulting in my being in my present predicament.

After the steamer had left the city limits, the view of the shorelines' natural beauty became more and more apparent as the images of the city's destruction receded. My spirits were raised by the bright sun and the soft green foliage aligning the Elbe. The sight of Blankenese brought sheer joy; passing the Süllberg brought back memories of our arrival in Hamburg via the S.S. Roosevelt. I prayed for a speedy departure to cross the ocean back home to New York, and to once again see the Statue of Liberty.

When I debarked in Borstel, I was met by an enthusiastic, hazel-eyed teacher. Fräulein Gertrud Schmidt had come to the ferry landing by bicycle. My violin and only suitcase were slung onto the bike. Frl. Schmidt determinately pushed it along the road to York, while I marched along next to her. My offers to relieve her were declined dogmatically. "Don't worry, I expect to have much for you to do later," she said brightly. I shrugged my shoulders, and did not pursue the matter further. She quizzed me about my American birth, volunteering admiration for the English language, and continued our conversation in that tongue. She had a clipped British accent, which she had acquired while studying in England. We traversed a series of gently sloping dikes which extended for miles parallel to the Elbe. Between the dikes, a system of ditches provided drainage for the orchards which had been planted to take advantage of the fertile soil created by the occasional flooding of the river in years gone by. The rich fruit marshland was now heavy with its crop, waiting to be picked. "Tomorrow, we will all be busy bringing in the harvest," Frl. Schmidt announced. "Our destination now is to the local physician's house, where I am lodged. His wife, a former nurse, is taking care of his practice, since he has been drafted." I was invited to join them for dinner. As in Frehne, women reigned domestically. The doctor's wife became the head of the household, however, as a physician's assistant, she had been able to take over only part of his medical duties, leaving the area with limited medical services. She had been provided, as was the custom, with domestic and child care help by the regime. Frl. Schmidt introduced her to me as Frau Doktor, and my eyes widened as Frl. Schmidt winked, shrugging her shoulders.

After supper, I was brought to my new foster home. Frau Huber was the antithesis of my former rifle-toting ranger's wife in the rural Prignitz. She was a beautiful, well groomed and polished business woman, who ran her own drug store with the help of a 20 year old apprentice. It was actually a mini-mall complex, consisting of the store, a barber shop, a beauty parlor, and a photographer's darkroom. The barber was her father-in-law, the parlor was operated by hired help, and she operated the darkroom. Herr Huber, who had also been drafted, had left his business in the capable hands of his wife, who was both a professional druggist and photographer. This was not a pharmacy or apothecary, which in Germany are entirely separate businesses. An *Arbeitsdienst Mädchen* named Ria took care of the two Huber toddler girls, as well as doing the cooking for all of us. In the evening, Ria went home to stay in the apartment set aside for the jailer of the town, Ria's father, who had passed away before I had come to town. Her mother and sister, who lived with her, had taken over the duties of maintaining the town prison in the absence of her father. The tiny 4-cell jail, with its enclosed landscaped courtyard, was very quaint, and never housed an inmate during my stay in York.

I slept in a small attic room on the third floor of the Huber building, in the customary feather bed. The rest of the time, I was able to spend with the Huber family when not attending school. Our *Oberbau* education was set up in the modern facilities of a local school and gymnasium. 28 girls were provided with 5 teachers and the ubiquitous Hitler Youth leader. My curriculum was expanded, and my music lessons augmented by playing second fiddle to Frl. Schmidt, who also was a violinist. I had arrived in time to participate in the harvest of the large, dark cherries. We also later aided in the picking of plums of various colors and sizes, finishing off the season of the fruit belt country of *das Alte Land* with the winter apples. Many years ago, only fishermen had lived along these banks, but since the mouth of the Elbe is quite wide along these shores, precious soil had been won from the river by building the dike system. Resourceful, clever, hard working inhabitants had started planting fruit trees in the drained-off fields between the embankments, lacing the orchards with drainage canals. They had become the wealthiest fruit farmers in this region, living in beautiful and very ornate brick decorated farm houses in stoic splendor.

Frl. Nölting, our German literature teacher, had taken us to the fruit orchard. While all of us were picking, she sang this song, dedicating it to me:

> *Tillah reiste mit Papa, dem es riesig freut-*
> *Reise Ziel Amerika, Linie Bremer Lloyd.*
> *Eine pracht Kabine stand für Sie reserviert,*
> *aber ach! Es war die Wand rötlich tapeziert.*
> *Zu dem Steward spricht entsetzt die schöne Tillah-*
> *Nein, nicht Rot, Rot mach' ich nicht,*
> *bitte Lillah, bitte Lillah*
> *bitte Lillah la la la, Lillah la la la la!*

The song had many more stanzas, about the heroin Tillah, who traveled to America with her father in a Bremer Lloyd steamer cabin with red colored walls. She, however, detested red, and made a great fuss about insisting on lavender. It was rather ironic that my first Bethpage, Long Island school teachers were named Miss Lilac and Miss Orcette, and lavender was really one of my favorite colors. I was again wearing my Hitler Youth blouse and skirt, which were becoming rather shabby and worn, for my fruit picking chores. Although this greatly annoyed the youth leader, my teacher facetiously remarked how pleased the Führer would be to see me wearing the uniform for work. Sure enough, the next time I saw the leader, she gifted me with a brand new official white blouse. This augmented my meager wardrobe, and I frequently wore it to school, however with a plaid skirt. Since I now lodged in a small town business establishment, I did not have to change my manner from my city demeanor. My extra chores consisted in helping Ria in the kitchen, or baby sitting the two adorable girls. When Frau Huber had a large batch of photo prints to process, I would assist by trimming the edges of the pictures with a special hand cutter, which created the ornate effects in vogue at the time. It was a pleasant household, with visits from my foster mother's parents. Her father was the bureaucrat in charge of rationing cards and *An- und Abmeldescheine*. The latter were special passes which permitted the bearer to remain or leave the town.

My pocket money was spent on weekly shampoos and sets, toiletries from Frau Huber's shop, movies, or church. The tenacious BDM leader was again annoyed with my appearing at youth rallies with polished finger nails, perfume, or garish beads and fluttering ribbons adorning my official white blouse. I was ordered to eliminate my adornments, which simply resulted in my not attending any more of her meets.

Mama wrote that Papa had finished his army training in Holland, and had been transferred back to the Submarine Base. An attic apartment at the Neuhof block, ten minutes from his place of work, had been made available for the family. They had then moved from the Deichstrasse to Neuhof in the submarine Freeharbor district. My classmates and I were taking lessons from the local Pastor to study for Confirmation. The Pastor was enthralled with my American baptism certificate, which I had received from the Seamen's Church in Manhattan. He asked to retain the large and elaborate document to show to some of his colleagues. Unfortunately, the dress my mother had received as a gift from Tallulah Bankhead while my father had worked at Gracie Square, and which she had saved for me to wear at my confirmation, had been destroyed in the bombings. I had received several yards of coarse navy blue material for my birthday, which Frau Huber arranged to be made into a dress pattern of my choice by the local seamstress. In March of 1945, I slipped into the long-sleeved, circular-skirted dress, and pinned a fake spray of Lilly-of-the-valley corsage to the pleated top, and was ready for the important event. I was startled to find the inscription *"Der Herr ist treu; Der wird Euch stärken und bewahren vor dem Argen"* in my certificate. When I read it, my heart skipped a beat, bringing tears to my eyes. I recalled the very words my grandmother had uttered after our bible sessions in her home. My parents, sister Erika, Frl. Schmidt, Frau Huber, and Ria attended not only the services, but a party celebration which had been arranged by my foster mother for all of us. Papa wore the uniform of a field soldier, having received special permission to leave Hamburg for this event. He still had not sewn on his newly earned PFC stripe, and I jestingly offered to do the honors. Mama proudly told me of the decorating she had done to the cheerful attic apartment, which had a spectacular view of the Freeharbor waterfront. Sadly, in the next letter I received from her, she told of the results of another air raid. While in the shelter, neighbors had informed Papa that the roof of our apartment was burning. He rushed up to try to extinguish the flames, but sadly found that all of our furniture, clothing, and the new radio had been stolen. I wept in frustration and fury.

While we were taking lessons with him, our geometry teacher gave us a special assignment, which was to determine the height of the York church steeple mathematically. Since science and math were my nemesis, and my friend Elfriede was not there to help me, I was on my own with this problem. Being embarrassed to ask for help from some of the smarter girls, I recruited one of my music fans to help. Armed with a makeshift plumb line and a broomstick, I climbed into the belfry. I lowered the plumb to the ground, tied a knot in the line at the level of the belfry window, and dropped the line for my waiting classmate to physically measure. Then I precariously hung out of the tower window, and raised the broomstick as high as I could reach. My assistant moved away to a position which permitted her to estimate the number of broomstick lengths required to reach the spire. Mr. Squaremeter, the nickname I had given the math teacher, was astonished at the accuracy of the figure we arrived at for the height of the structure. We, of course, chose not to divulge the devious means we had employed to ascertain our answer, but the jig was up when he insisted on seeing our computations.

RIA HAD BECOME my confidant, and she heard most of my lamenting about injustice. After the noon meal, while sharing the cleanup chores, we would talk. One afternoon while in the Huber kitchen, Ria was all smiles. Her large brown eyes were dancing more than usual. "Wait 'till you hear this!" she whispered while we carried the dishes out of the dining room. Quietly, she closed the kitchen door. She pulled a letter from her apron pocket, and waved it in front of my face. Ria had received it from the headquarters of the Gestapo, she confided to me. The hair at the nape of my neck rose in fear, but I stayed calm, and just listened to her conversation. "They want me to fill out a long questionnaire," she volunteered. "What sort of questions?" I asked suspiciously. "Oh, vital statistics, such as my height, weight, and color of my hair." "Why?" I inquired. "Because my friend has leave, and I am going to become engaged to an S.S. man," she beamed. I relaxed, and congratulated her. "He's coming next week," she exclaimed joyously. "My mother and sister are going to have an afternoon *Kaffee Klatsch*, and I want you to come to meet him."

Since my daily contacts were mostly with women, old men, very young boys, or *vertrocknete Akademiker*, as we called our male teachers, I was indeed curious to meet Ria's beau. I inwardly asked myself how come he gets leave, not Herr Huber, or the Frau Dokter's, or the grocery lady's husbands? Most of the business women in York were friends, meeting for weekly gossip sessions in each other's homes. I would stay in my room and read or go for a walk when they came to the Huber household. I was thinking of the aversion the S.S. symbol evoked in me. Now I was to meet one in a social situation. We had covered the history of Frederick William I, father of Frederick the Great, who was the builder of

Prussian power. His hobby had been the collection of tall soldiers for his personal body guard. The S.S., or *Schutz Staffel*, was formed to be the elite guard in the present regime. I wondered what sort of person Ria's fiancé would be. That Sunday afternoon, I preened more than usual in front of the mirror, but suddenly stopped. I covered my blond hair carefully with a kerchief. *Die grosse, blonde Hamburgerin* had become my thumbnail description, and I was afraid that the Teutonic appearance might make me a candidate for exploitation by the Third Reich. History lessons had made me leery of the intentions of any kind of authority trickling down from a land which I regarded as not being representative of my ideal government. Being familiar with the moves of chessboard figures, I always imagined myself as merely a pawn trying to reach the other side of the board, which in my mind, was America. When I reached it, I would be entitled to promotion. The process of promoting is known as queening a pawn. Upon reaching the eighth row, a pawn is exchanged for any chess piece of its own color, except a king. The queen can move freely, and that is what I hoped to be able to do. Slowly, I walked the short distance to the town jail where Ria lived. I was shocked to see a tired, weary looking man with sad eyes. He could have been used as the model for a portrait of despair. "He is recuperating from war wounds," Ria said sympathetically.

FRL. SCHMIDT WAS not only my teacher and violin partner, but had become a friend and confidant as well. Several students knew that we practiced our instruments together, but none of them were aware of our political and philosophical discussions. Since Frl. Schmidt had studied in Great Britain, we often had our conversations in English. Her views were not the dogmatic ones of the NSDAP (National Socialist German Worker's Party). The party lapel button which all teachers were obligated to wear did not reflect her personal convictions. She augmented our prescribed curriculum with more universal history than was standard. "The people of ancient Greece were the first to develop a democratic way of life, more than 2000 years ago," she would innocently begin the lesson, glancing briefly in my direction, "originating the idea that every citizen should take an active part in their government. Jefferson, an American president, stood for peace and Democracy; his simple ways emphasized the fact that government would then pay more attention to the common man. He cut government taxes, reduced the size of the navy, paid off much of the national debt, and tried hard to avoid war." "Our type of government, with a Führer at the head, is not the norm," she added bravely. "We are in a very bad war situation, as you all know, and every man , woman, and child is suffering because of it." For many in my grade, her words were just part of the daily, ordinary lesson plan, like so much water rolling off a duck's back. The cross section of thinking human beings tuned into an educational curriculum day after day, seems to have the same percentage of bright, enthusiastic participants, thoughtful, serious students, and a majority of partially comatose creatures filling up space in any classroom on either side of the Atlantic.

My annoying habit of asking questions, which had to be very actively curbed much of the time during the years I was living in Nazi Germany, was often commented upon. "She hasn't learned that lesson," my mother would say in that direct way, which managed to combine grimness with humor. "Keep your mouth shut! Just listen, but do not comment." I really hated that bit of advice, but never went against any disciplinary suggestions coming from my parents. I instinctively knew that many of their decisions and actions were correct for our survival. I, as a child, was as powerless to persuade them as it was to argue against the political regime that engulfed us all. The underlying current between my family and me was always: why did we have to live in this war-torn country, when New York was my home town? Verbal accusations were never made, but the rift of not having put up more of a protest to stay in the United States was often magnified in my own mind. Dealing with a tyrannical bureaucracy controlling every aspect of one's life was a constant reminder of the freedom of choice I thought was so evident in my own country. My mother often told me how she had asked for help from her previous employers, several of whom had influential positions in the New York State government, to no avail. "Where there's a will, there's a way," I would shout impatiently. However, I had learned that bureaucracies within governments often acted with little or no compassion. Each department jealously guarded its power by acting in a dictatorial manner suitable to its own agenda. Mama was a courageous diplomat during her Rathhaus visits, when the clerks demanded advance taxes. She had to bring the tariff regardless of her protests, and Papa was given lots of overtime to repair the iron coffins. The U-boat bunker, with the vast steel gate open to the Neuhof arm of the Elbe, was receiving a change of the Wolf Pack fleet, which consisted of teams of three to fifteen subs acting in attack unison in the North Atlantic. The Allied Nations had developed additional convoy techniques to meet the submarine challenge. The development of Radar and Sonar had provided new ways of locating the U-boats, and the procession of limping "sardine cans", as my father called them, gave him constant work. Many subs did not make it back to the vast shelter. The *Unterseeboote,* or U-boats for short, were one of Germany's major weapons.

My mother, sister, and I, as dependents of a vital defense industry worker, were allowed to take shelter in the U-boat bunker during air raids. We would crouch between the overhead cranes, huddled together with other neighbors from the Neuhof block. Like us, they were families of the base workers who lived in the housing project on the peninsula that was part of the free harbor shipbuilding complex. I only had brief terrifying hours in this bunker, burying my head in a pillow or blanket during the skip-bombing raids when the Allied planes were directly targeting the submarine base. On one such attack, the power supply to the pen gate lost electricity. The gate was only partially closed, and I could plainly observe the efforts of the pilots trying to skip-bomb their lethal cargoes into the pool pen, to destroy the long, dark U-boats lying like large, slender whales next to each other. My sister and mother saw sailors as well as civilians being killed all around them, and reported these events to me during one of my brief vacation times with them. However, just as soldiers on leave recuperating from wounds experienced, cities, and especially submarine bases, were not ideal places to seek shelter during a war. Therefor, my parents decided that I should stay in York with my teachers and classmates.

The day before my January 31st, 1945 birthday, the *Wilhelm Gustloff*, one of the KdF Dampfer (steamships) that I had admired while it was berthed along the pier at the Hamburg Landungsbrücken was being used to rescue refugees from East Prussia. Since the Soviet offensive on January 12th, the people were fleeing to the west in minus 20 degree Celsius temperatures to the harbors of Pillau, Gotenhafen, and Kolberg,, near Danzig, to escape the terror of the Red Army. Of the 6,100 fleeing , many of whom were wounded, 5000 drowned in the Baltic after having been torpedoed by the Russians. Thousands more died, victims of the sinking of the Lloyd-Dampfer *General von Steuben,* and on April 16th, the Hapag-Motorschiff *Goya.*

On January 17th, over 250 U.S. planes again carpet bombed the Hamburg harbor industrial area where my parents and sister were living. It continued on with my beloved *Theater an der Reeperbahn* (Operetta house) being completely destroyed, and the St. Michael's church suffering heavy damage. On April 29th, the last low flying bombers destroyed the *Thalia* theater.

MY ROLE MODELS were strong women, but my career goals had been influenced by both sexes. One of the first by sailors, merchant seamen, that is; I fantasized being a navigator on the largest ocean liner afloat. Marga von Herringen was the beautiful woman dentist who cared for my sister's and my own teeth in Altona, and for a while, a picture of my very own dental office was on my mind. The practice of pulling and drilling, however, exhausted me in my pretending. Uncle Hans was an opera buff. Eagerly, I embraced the spectacle of the grandest of theater, having had early exposure to this art form at the New York Metropolitan Opera. At the Lahrmannstrasse, the gypsy Opa's lovely serenades had touched my heart, and kindled the spark of my choice of the violin. Even though I worked hard at practicing this very difficult instrument, I realized that I did not have the talent or complete dedication required of a virtuoso. When I was ten years of age, my American Indian silver ring had lost its turquoise stone. My lamenting to a goldsmith two houses from the lady dentist got me a tour of his establishment. A complete new world of craftsmanship was opened to me. When I came back to the shop with designs for replacements, the proprietor offered me an apprenticeship in jewelry design when I was finished with school. These were a few of the opportunities influencing a possible choice of careers. The acquisition of home management skills for the survival of the family unit were taken for granted. If one is fortunate enough to live in a household where one breadwinner is enough to supply the financial needs of the unit, fine, if not, the chores and responsibilities must be divided among all members of the family. The subtle, but forceful messages for girls to be passive and submissive, is the irrational hope of some parents and teachers who have a chained idea of their own worth. Yet, a realistic self-appraisal of the entire human being is essential to career planning. One's choice at age fourteen will have been augmented or changed in schooling, trade involvement, and of availability of employment many times before life's end due to social and economic influences. Also, the mental, physical, and emotional makeup of a boy or girl must be considered.

MY MOTHER'S CAREER as a nurse or nanny for the wealthy influenced me greatly to realize that the job of raising children is a fulltime occupation. The German educational regime was fully aware of that importance. Once the elementary schooltime was completed by the majority of students, they were pressed into the *Arbeitsdienst*. For girls, that meant that they were to be disbursed to households of professional women who needed assistance to run their homes. Boys were sent to semi-military duty in work details. Ria was for me a role model in the running of a household, while Frau Huber tended to her business as a druggist and photographer. On Sundays, when the shop was closed, I helped my foster mother take on the job of food preparation, allowing her to spend quality time with her two girls, and Ria could enjoy the day with her own family. But for the war, it would have been an ideal small town life.

Distant cannon or artillery fire could now be regularly heard. That morning, announcements by radio and local newspapers warned people to stay off the streets because prisoners of war were to be marched along the roads on their way to Hamburg. Of course, the regime did not say what nationality the prisoners were. Frau Huber and I looked out of the livingroom window. Hundreds of captured soldiers were being guided through York by only a handful of German guards. *"Halt! Zwanzig Minuten Pause!"* the German officer shouted. Within minutes, the throng melted out of the march formation. Crouched or squatted uniformed men were draped casually across steps, store fronts, curbs, and in front of the Huber's establishment as far as the eye could see, in a manner which immediately suggested to me that they were Americans. Excitedly, I ran outside to speak to some of them, and to perhaps hear some recent and real news uncensored by the Nazi propaganda machine. I was thrilled to be told that Allied forces were not far away, and that it seemed quite probable that the war would soon come to an end. Strangely enough to my experience, one of the Yanks offered me a piece of chocolate, which I had not enjoyed for several years.

Last Days of the War

The very brief conversation with a group of American prisoners of war gave me an insight to the decision I had to make. Frl. Schmidt told me of leaflets being dropped on Hamburg warning against resistance. "American and British planes are ready to totally destroy the city if there is any resistance on the part of the population", my teacher reported to me. "If the citizens chose to fight, ...", her voice trailed off. "I'm leaving for Hamburg!" I calmly said to her. She looked at me for what seemed an eternity. "You will need your rationing cards, *Meldeschein,* and *Ausweis*." I heard Frl.Schmidt say. I nodded. "Frau Huber's father can supply me with all the necessary papers; I should have no problem getting everything in order." By the late afternoon, I had a stack of documents to add into my one suitcase. I folded all together with my American birth certificate, other New York City health and Bethpage school report cards, adding them to the York confirmation papers, plus a few photos. After my confirmation, the pastor had died. I again went to the parsonage to try to get my New York baptism document back, but the woman there said that she had no authority to return my beautiful Seamen's Church certificate. I never got it back!

Frau Huber suggested that I take my suitcase with all my belongings and the required papers to her friend's ferry station house in Borstel by bicycle the night before my planned departure to Hamburg. "Tomorrow morning, when you leave, I will give you a basket of winter apples to take along to your folks back home. You can carry that plus your violin." Of course, that was a very practical idea. I thanked Frau Huber for her support. Frl. Schmidt pedaled along side me while I pushed Frau Huber's borrowed bike with the suitcase slung over the handlebars. When we arrived, we chatted for a few minutes with the keeper of the station, and she assured me that my valise would be safe with her until I came for it in the morning to take the steam ferry into Hamburg. Frl. Schmidt and I each cycled back to York, and bid each other a solemn *Auf Wiedersehen.* I thanked her for all the help she had given me with my academic and musical studies. "I hope to see you in Hamburg when the war ends." To this day, I am surprised that she never questioned my decision to leave the relative safety of the area to enter the dangerous combat zone. She respected my judgement in wanting to be with my family, and perhaps even to die together.

Early the following morning, the main street was quiet and foggy. I set off to the river boat station carrying my violin and the large basket of apples. A farmer perched uneasily on the wooden seat of a buckboard halted his horse to ask about my destination. "The morning boat to Hamburg," I replied. "No ferries or ships of any kind are permitted on the Elbe. The British will be coming soon," he said. He reiterated the warnings about the dangers of resistance, and the threats of total destruction of the city should the population in any way oppose the entrance of the British troops. Before I could really decide what to do, a German military truck approached us at great speed. It came to a screeching halt in front of us, and the driver leaped out of the cab. Hungrily eyeing my basket of apples, he asked where I was headed. I told him that I was hoping to join my parents in Hamburg to be with them when the end came.

"Hop on, we too want to be with our families in Schleswig-Holstein. We can drop you off at the Hamburg *Bahnhof.*" I was helped up to the back of the open truck with my violin and basket of apples. There, huddled together were a half dozen very young German soldiers. They were a sorry looking lot, gaunt, morose, and obviously hungry. I offered them some of the apples, which they also passed along to the driver and passenger up front. We drove along at a furious pace, and as we approached the locale of the ferry station, I began trying to get the attention of the driver. By the time I succeeded, we were well passed it, and the driver shouted back that they would not be able to back up to drop me off. I fatalistically resigned myself to proceeding to Hamburg without my suitcase.

Grimly, we continued at a frantic speed. We were now on the open road on the way to the Hamburger *Chaussee*, with fields, trees, and small brush enveloped by a light, cold morning mist. Suddenly, the roar of a low flying fighter plane startled us. The driver swerved off the road just in time to avoid a volley of machine gun fire erupting along the road. We all dove off the truck to land in the bushes at the side of the road. It all happened so fast, that we could not see if the plane was German or Allied, and luckily, the truck , although riddled, was still able to operate. My violin had also survived without damage. We clambered aboard again after assuring ourselves that the aircraft would not return, and resumed our hair-raising speed. As we approached the outskirts of the city, mounds of rubble on either side of the road presaged the terrible and appalling destruction which became visible as we neared the city center. A pall of gloom descended upon all of us in the truck. With mutual wishes of good luck, I was dropped off at the *Hamburger Hauptbahnhof*. I entered the train station to find the ladies room and clean myself of the dirt and mud covering me as a result of my ordeal. People were walking about the damaged city, and miraculously, some trains were leaving and arriving. I was fortunate to find a toilet that still had a cold water faucet that was still operating. My handkerchief, which I had wrapped around my wallet and comb, was used as a washcloth, and the dish towel covering the apples served as a hand towel.

It is said, that there often is a fine line between teen bravado and teen depression, and now, as I saw my reflection in the restroom mirror, I scarcely could recognize myself. Again, as I had years ago, when arriving from New York City, I started to talk to myself. In retrospect, I realized that my youth was shrouded in constant challenges. Now, it would be to survive the end of this war. The toilet maintenance lady came clanging into the area with her pails, and she was astonished to find a violin student. "Are you going to fiddle while Hamburg burns?" she remarked drily. I laughed in spite of my morose mood, and gave her an apple as a tip for the use of the facilities.

Winding my way through the wreckage bordering the streets, I searched in vain for any form of public transportation to the harbor. It took me an hour to reach the warehouse district, and immediately upon my arrival, the sirens sounded an air alarm. I took refuge in one of the nearby round bunkers, which we all were painfully aware were not built to withstand the most recent blockbusters. A gray mass of humanity filed silently into the emergency-lit shelter. A mother, with her infant cradled in her arms, sat next to me. When the baby whimpered, she tried to sooth it with words, but finally had to nurse it. The woman was pale and undernourished, and the child had to suck hard for satisfaction. "I don't have any more milk for you," she whispered. We could hear the planes roaring overhead, but to our immense relief, did not hear the dreaded vibrations of exploding bombs. I gave the woman an apple from my now sadly depleted basket, which she accepted with many thanks and blessings. After the all-clear sounded, I set out again for the *Landungsbrücken*. At the ferry station, I was told how fortunate I was to be able to find a small craft which would take me to the *Neuhof* peninsula. The *Harburg* paddle wheel ferry, which I normally would board, lay unattended at its pier. The round-trip ferries, or so-called *Jollenführer*, were frequently used whenever I could not catch the *Harburg* ferry to either leave from the Hamburg pier to sail to or from the *Neuhof* peninsula. The captain of the ferry was a jolly fellow, and seemed to remember me from previous trips, though they had been months ago. "Why are you going to *Neuhof*? Weren't you sent away to a safer place to attend school?" he inquired. Then he joked: "Or perhaps you have come to fiddle while Hamburg burns?" I was now beginning to feel foolish about having decided to leave my tranquil sanctuary at York. As we motored along the waterways of the harbor, we passed acres of church bells of all sizes and shapes which lay strewn along the shore, and had been collected for the war effort from all over Germany. They subsequently lay there, well after the war's end, often covered in ice and snow, for years before being returned to their rightful places.

RESIDING IN THE housing block of *Neuhof* was like living in a small town. Everybody knew who you were, everybody knew who walked with or talked to you. It was both good and bad. The worst thing about that was, we also knew who the Gestapo man of the block was, as well as felt his constant surveillance. I now wondered what my parents would say when I arrived at the Nippoldstrasse attic apartment. Apprehensively, I climbed the five flights of stairs. I knocked on the door, and my mother's face immediately told me how wrong I had been to have left the Huber household. "What are you doing here? Where is your suitcase?" she blurted out. When I told her that it was at the Borstel ferry station, and the circumstances of my decision, she calmed down a bit. "Wait till your father comes home!" she said grimly. "He always told you to keep your American birth certificate with you at all times. Gee, how could you be so careless?" She was shaking her head. "Then, of course, your *Ausweis*, *Meldeschein*, and ration cards. You cannot function without them, and I cannot even feed you!" She continued on and on, while my sister sat silently in the corner on the attic window seat, drawing.

When Papa came home from the submarine base around five o'clock, another barrage of recriminations were launched on me. "My god, what are we going to do?" he said, half to himself and to us. Then he became quiet, and started pacing the floor. After several minutes, he turned to my mother and said, "Get my dark turtle neck sweater, navy pants and jacket, Martha. You, Helen, write a note to Whom It May Concern, for the attendants at the *Borstel* ferry station, so they will give me your suitcase." My mother already knew in a flash what his intentions were, and begged him not to leave *Neuhof*. "Your *Ausweis* restricts you to the city of Hamburg. If you are caught outside of the area, it may be considered an act of espionage. No, Eric, don't go!" She was near to tears, and so was I. What had I done?

Papa had made up his mind, and said, "We need that suitcase!" He then calmly ate some of the soup my mother had prepared, and one of the apples I had brought. Having made his plans and eaten, he went into the bedroom, and napped until it was dark. He later emerged wearing his dark navy clothes, put another apple into his coat pocket, and bid us a solemn goodby. My mother walked down the stairs with him, to where he had stored his bicycle. After carefully making certain that the black garbed Gestapo man was not in sight, he planned to pedal to his tugboat captain friend, and borrow a rowboat. He then would cross the *Süder Elbe* with the bicycle on board. After carefully hiding the boat, he planned to cycle to *Borstel* to retrieve my suitcase. However, we knew that the waterfront was everywhere under constant searchlight surveillance. Would he even reach the opposite shore without being detected?

"Why did you leave York?" Erika asked me. "We all were glad that you were living in a safe place," she continued. "Mama has a hard time feeding us, and now you're here without your ration cards." She put on an all-knowing face, that only a kid sister knew how to do. "At the last air raid damage we wrote to you about, when the neighbors came to put out the fire, they stole our radio that Papa had just gotten by trading his six month cigarette supply. Helen, he never smokes anymore! Mama's and his cigarette ration are always traded for food." Just then, my mother returned. She had pulled down the window darkening material before she had gone downstairs, but now put out the one lamp in our kitchen/ living room area, and rolled up the black paper covering the skylight window. The three of us then stood on a bench to have a view of the area surrounding the submarine base and the Elbe waterways. We saw several searchlights regularly scanning the area. We stood silently watching. My legs started to become numb, and my stomach began to rumble. "Let's go to bed," Mama finally said. Erika shared her bedroom with me. We each had a single bed, and we shared one bookcase. All my clothes and belongings were still in the suitcase that Papa was now hoping to retrieve for me.

Erika soon fell asleep, but I found sleep elusive. The moonlight shining through the uncovered skylight gave a surrealistic air to my musings. How could I have been so thoughtless? Why, indeed, did I ever leave York? Did I expect my parents to welcome me with open arms? My father was always somewhere between a rock and a hard place, he used to say. Deported from the U.S.A. for the lack of the proper documentation, even though I and my sister had been born in New York, was for me, a most unfair and evil deed for a government. I learned at an early age that regimes often make very unwise laws. I will have to try to changed that, but for the moment, how can I make up for the grief I caused the family? While I lay there silently berating myself, I noticed a movement on the bed of my sleeping sister. To my shock, I could barely make out the shape of a large rat creeping up towards her pillow. Not daring to cry out, I watched in amazement as the creature snuggled up to her head, lying itself down on her hair which lay across the pillow, and quietly go to sleep. My thoughts slowly turned to my father. How long will it take him to cross the *Süder Elbe*, and then pedal to *Borstel* and back? Finally, I drifted off to sleep in the early morning hours. A loud knock on our apartment door awakened me. I had gone to bed wearing my underwear and dress, which my mother and sister also commonly did, to be prepared to just throw on a hat and coat if the air alarm should sound. Mama went to the door, and found her friend Frau Winkler standing there holding out a paper. "Look here, leaflets have been distributed by the block warden. It seems that he found a large batch of them after the last air raid. He now feels that we had better heed their warning!" We gathered around Frau Winkler. She read the large print on the flyer: Give up without resistance! Do not harm our occupation troops when they march into Hamburg! We all took a deep breath while Mama heated the *ersatz* coffee, which would be our only breakfast. Frau Winkler voiced her concern about her neighbor, *die alte, verrückte Oma*. I remembered this crazy old woman, who constantly cursed the pilots of the Allied bombers, and threatened to boil them alive if she could ever get her hands on them. She now extended her threats to include any of the occupation troops that might pass by under her windows. Frau Winkler said, "We must do something about her when the troops march in, or else she may bring destruction upon us all. The British troops are already close to Bremen." My mother, sister, and I were stunned at her disclosures.

WE WAITED FOR two days and nights for Papa to return. Finally, we heard his special knock on the door. He came in looking totally exhausted, threw the suitcase at my feet, and swatted me across the face. "Here, you nearly got me killed!" was all he shouted, and went into the bedroom with my mother. Erika and I sat in shocked silence. After what seemed like hours, my mother came into the room. "Papa is sleeping, and he will be O.K.," is all she volunteered. I decided to go for a walk, which had been my habit for years. I always found that *Spazierengehen* refreshed my body and mind. I would be seen by the neighbors who knew my family, who my friends were, and would hear them whisper, *"Die Amerikanerin"* as I strolled by. On *Neuhof,* the rumor mill that follows is often inaccurate, but efficient. The Gestapo spy saw me, and I could feel his beady eyes boring into my back as I passed him and his police dog on my way to the old fishing cottages along the waterfront. I watched a fishing *Ewer* sail up to the beach. The fisherman's wife was helping to skin the eels of his catch. She threw them onto the sand to enable her to get a grip on them. Quickly and efficiently, from many years of practice, her task was done. I admired her skill. "Do you like eel?" she asked. "Of course," I answered, "I'm always hungry." She wrapped a still wiggling small one into a piece of newspaper, and handed it to me. "I don't have any money with me, and nothing to trade for it," I remember saying. *"Guten Appetit!"* was all she said, busying herself further on her husband's boat.

HELEN H. BUCHHOLTZ

On my way back to the housing block, I met the sister of one of Erika's friends. Helga was her name, and she seemed glad to see me. I told her about my having left my school group, but that I now had realized my mistake. "I have to find some way of getting some extra food items without using my ration cards, to make up for the trouble I have caused my parents. "Do you have any ideas?" She said that she would try to come up with some alternatives, and come by in the morning. When I returned home, my mother had cooked a soup. I proudly handed her the eel to prepare for my father, as I knew that, in spite of the extreme shortage of foods, neither she nor my sister would eat it. She had taken all my clothes out of the suitcase, doubling the dresses, blouse, and skirt on the few hangers we possessed. She then proceeded to tell me an account of my father's harrowing adventure. He had been caught by a German army patrol after he had successfully retrieved my suitcase from the *Borstel* ferry station. They had searched through the suitcase, and when they had discovered my American documents, they had branded him a spy, believing that my clothes were some kind of disguise. He was then locked up in the basement of the local army headquarters, to be executed the following day. All night, he heard the officer pacing the floor above my father's cell. Papa had resigned himself to his fate. However, the *Oberst* came down the following morning carrying the neatly repacked suitcase, unlocked the cell door, and said, "The war will be over within the next few days. Go, and good luck to you!" I was in shock, and then started to cry in relief. No wonder Papa had been so angry!

Fatalism, British Occupation, and Law Apprentice

The next morning, Erika and I stood on the bench to look over the submarine base. People were coming from the free harbor area with bags, bundles, and baskets. "Look, they are coming out of the supply arsenal," Erika pointed out. She knew the layout of the various buildings better than I.

Just then, there was a knock on the door. It was Helga. "Are you ready?" she asked. "Take a basket, net, or bag to carry stuff in. We may already be too late," she lamented. "No man's land has been in effect for hours. Let's go, Helen!"

Mama and Papa were still sleeping. I turned to Erika. "Tell them I will be back as soon as possible, hopefully with some food."

Erika nodded, and closed the apartment door behind us. We hurried down the stairs, and when we reached the front of the apartment house entrance, I saw Frau Winkler pass by. She was carrying canned goods stuffed into blue and white checkered pillow cases, one in each hand. I asked where she had come from, and she told me she had been to the supply bunker of the *Marine Arsenal*.

"What about the crazy Oma, do you think we should keep an eye on her?" she called to me.

Helga and I helped Frau Winkler carry her loot up to her second floor apartment next door to our building. The deranged woman lived next door to her. Frau Winkler knocked on that door. A wild eyed, gaunt hag opened the door a crack. "How are you? What are you doing today?" Frau Winkler asked quietly.

"I'm getting ready to throw water and rocks out of my window!" she shrieked.

We pushed the door open, and gently guided the old lady into her kitchen. Sure enough, several pots and kettles of water stood in readiness on the stove. Near the front windows, facing the street, she had stored a large pile of rocks.

"I'm ready for the invasion forces," she cackled.

Only now did I really see how much of a threat this poor soul represented to all of us. Frau Winkler calmly tried to reason with her, to no avail. We all tacitly realized that it would have been disastrous to leave her to her wild schemes.

"Let's tie her to her chair," Frau Winkler whispered to us. "I'll look in on her every few hours until the danger is over."

We found a length of clothes line and quickly tied her to her arm chair, making her as comfortable as we could. Helga and I then continued on our quest, toward the supply center. Hordes of people were coming towards us, all carrying various articles. Helga and I looked at one another, realizing that we probably were already too late to reap any bounty, but we continued at an increasing pace.

That May morning of 1945 is clearly etched in my memory. We had reached the gate which was usually heavily guarded, but no sentry was to be seen. We saw that the huge metal doors had been thrown wide open. I heard men's voices echoing from afar, and then laughter. I cautiously glanced about, but saw noone, and then urged Helga onward to see if we could still possibly find something which would be of some use to us.

The sunlight streamed though the wide opening as we entered the huge bunker supply building. It took our eyes several moments to adjust to the dark interior, for all generators had been shut down. Then we both became aware of the massive destruction of the remaining food supplies. Everything that the previous raiders had not been able to carry off had been wantonly destroyed. Canned goods had been smashed, sacks of legumes mixed with sugar and salt, jars of preserves thrown against the walls, and drums of molasses had been punctured and allowed to drip onto linens and blankets.

We were appalled at the spitefulness of our neighbors. I kept repeating, *"Warum?"* Why, indeed!

Helga and I began sobbing out of frustration as we searched through the mess for anything salvageable and edible. I was fortunate to stumble across several partially spoiled blue and white checkered sheets which I rolled up and put into my net.

We continued to search for any kind of food stuff which was not contaminated with broken glass or sullied beyond redemption. I carefully picked some dried potatoes out of a half spilled metal drum, and filled my sack. Then I came across a few cans still intact, but covered with gooey spilled jam. Our eyes had by now become accustomed to darkness which was only penetrated by the sunlight streaming through the tall warehouse doors.

We suddenly heard the clatter of heavy combat boots echoing on the concrete apron of the warehouse entrance. We saw the silhouettes of machine gun carrying soldiers outlined in the sunlit portals. We froze in fright. With a loud clatter, the sack of canned goods I was carrying dropped to the pavement. "Hands up, lassies!" one of them shouted. I was now shaking uncontrollably, but when I heard the Scottish burr, I shouted in return, "Stop scaring us, Scotty!"

The two soldiers lowered their weapons and began laughing loudly. Slowly and cautiously, we picked up what we had gathered. Helga then hid behind a partition. I did not want to go near the men. After much coaxing to come out of the warehouse by the one in the red beret, I persuaded Helga to accompany me in leaving. However, Scotty blocked our way, lecturing us about the wanton destruction. "We have to get food to England. They are starving there!" He went on and on, fancying himself to be the sole provider, and we the ones thwarting his plans.

It was even getting somewhat tedious for the redcap, and frightening for Helga, as she understood very little English. I had picked up the canned goods again, and I stuffed the dried potatoes on top of the sheets in the net sack. I then walked up to Scotty, dropped the canned goods in front of his feet, and managed to utter: "Here's a donation for the hungry English!" They courteously bowed and let us pass.

We were permitted to keep the rest of our meager booty. "Soon we will be celebrating our victory with you lassies!" Scotty shouted after us.

As we walked back to the housing block, some neighbors we met on the way urged us to hurry. It seemed that British troops of the seventh tank division, known as Desert Rats, were moving across the Elbe bridges. A few men we met had seen a ship, and asked us if we had seen any soldiers. Helga excitedly related our frightening experience. "Helen talked to them, and they lowered their weapons," she repeated several times. By the time we got to the Nippoldstrasse, I was a heroin to some, and an English collaborator to others, but what else could you expect from *der Amerikanerin*, I heard them whisper.

Before bringing my sparse offerings upstairs to my family, I climbed the stairs to the Winkler apartment landing. Frau Winkler had been watching my arrival from her window, and met me in the hall. "All is well with the old lady," she whispered. "I went to Frau Doktor, who gave me some sleeping pills for *die arme Frau*." I then showed her my two blue and white checkered sheets and dried potatoes, and related our experiences with the first Tommies to be seen on the sub base. She invited me into her kitchen for a cup of peppermint tea, and turned on her radio. "We are lucky to have electricity!" she said. I was eager to hear the latest news, since our radio had been stolen.

Reichsstatthalter Karl Kaufmann handed over the city to the occupation forces to spare the lives of hundreds of thousands of women and children, came the announcement from the Hamburg radio station. We sighed with relief, for we knew that he had been warned previous to the July 1943 massive air raids to evacuated the city, and had failed to do so, with the exception of his own family. The British panzer division would be entering the heart of the city via *Heidenkampsweg* and the *Mönckebergstrasse* to the *Rathaus*. I left Frau Winkler's apartment, and when I stepped into the street, I glanced to the right. There, I saw my father coming from the direction of the Free Harbor gate, which he used to get to his Howaldt workplace. I waited in the doorway, and jumped out as he came by, surprising him.

I related Helga's and my adventure to him, which he marveled at with the comment: *"Du hast mal wieder Glück gehabt!"* I certainly felt lucky. I then also related the Hamburg radio broadcast to him. Helping him with his two heavy canvas sacks, I lamented about my meager haul. "Never mind," my father interrupted. "When Erika told me that you were going to the submarine base, I decided to go to work." I laughed out loud. "We have no-man's land, no government, and Papa goes to his job! By the way, what is so heavy in these sacks? It feels like tools, Papa." He rested at the apartment house landing in front of our attic rooms, and carefully opened each bag. "Nobody was at our work station, and no guards were at the gate when I wanted to report for work," he smiled. "Now, look, I have tools again! I hope to make a deal down past the housing block for a piece of property to build a cottage for us." Proudly, he handed me each item to inspect. There was a hammer, a screw driver, a hand saw, a trowel, putty knife, axe, pry bar, and the prize item, a spirit level. Then, wrapped with sheets of sand paper, were two rat traps. When he saw the expression on my face as I looked at the traps, he asked me if I had seen any rats in the night. I then told him about the one I had seen sleeping near Erika. He reminded me that the disruption of the normal annual rat control procedures caused by the war had allowed the rat population to increase, and that some of the animals he had seen were quite large and frightening. He hoped that the traps would even be large enough.

The next day, only police were visible on the streets; the rest of the population remained in hiding as ordered, while the British forces moved across the Elbe bridges to the center of the city as reported. On the following day, mayor Kaufmann, as well as other

NSDAP functionaries and Hamburg bigwigs were arrested. We showed Mama and Erika our bounties. They were delighted to see us, as both had been worried by the orders spread house to house to stay indoors. Mama had prepared some soup, and Frau Kramer, the grocery store owner who occupied the right entrance area in our apartment complex for her shop, sold Mama the last loaf of bread from her stock. We all felt happy to be together, and relieved that Hamburg was not to be bombed in a last and futile battle of power. The end of this war was now finally in sight. However, we were too tired, emotionally and physically, to think of anything more than to have some uninterrupted sleep.

IN THE MEANTIME, British Brigadier General Douglas Spurling was negotiating from his battle position through the future military governor H. W. H. Armytage. The complete details and documentation for these events may be found in the German volume *Die Chronik Hamburgs*.

In the beginning of May, 1945, the passenger ships Cap Arcona and Thielbek, which housed seven thousand concentration camp victims were bombed by British fighter planes. Many died on board, burning to death, while others managed to dive into the water. A bitter fight for life rings, jackets, and wooden planks ensued, with only two hundred final survivors. The capitulation of Hamburg by Kaufmann was posted in the *Hamburger Zeitung* in the news office window *am Gänsemarkt*. Generalmajor Wolz, with three attendants, met with General Lewis D. Lyne and General Spurling near *Klecken*. These precedings were also reported by the Hamburg radio station. The British occupation forces chose the merchant Rudolf H. Petersen as the new *Bürgermeister* on May 15th. The most important task for the new mayor was the denazification of the city's management staff. On May 26th, Bruno Georges, who had been discharged from his position as police captain in 1933 by the Hitler regime, was reinstated as the head of the Hamburg police. 60 % of the police officials, 16% of teachers, 30% of university faculty, and 40% of the city bureaucrats did not return to work. I was quite happy to see that percentage of petty city clerks dismissed, remembering the long, long hours my mother and I had to stand in line to get approvals, permits, registrations, documentations to be taxed and stamped by these little caesars. The Allied forces celebrated their victory by turning on the air raid alarm sirens, and allowing them to howl for hours on end. When the war was officially declared over, we all went to bed. We slept for three days. When I awoke, I was ravenously hungry. "We now have to make plans for our survival against starvation," my father said to us.

Papa had remembered that after one of the waterfront bombings, the air pressure created by the bombs had pushed open the doors of the grain silos, and had blasted sacks of grain into the Elbe. Soon after the capitulation, when the population was again permitted onto the streets, he once more borrowed a rowboat from his friend. I was taken along to help in the recovery search. After rowing across the branch of the river towards the silos, Papa estimated the distance from shore he expected the sacks to have been blown, and dropped anchor. The water depth here averaged some 3 to 4 meters. Stripping down to his bathing suit, he slipped overboard, and began to dive and search the murky bottom for the sacks. After several hours of exhausting and unsuccessful attempts, he finally struck pay dirt. When he surfaced, I handed him the end of the rope we had brought along, and he dove to tie a loop around his find. He surfaced, climbed into the boat, and we both proceeded to haul up the very heavy grain sack, which now , in its water-soaked condition, weighed much more than its dry hundredweight. We could barely muster the energy to haul it aboard, but our dire needs gave us the extra bit of strength to succeed. After resting a while, Papa rowed us ashore to the pier where my mother and sister were anxiously waiting for us. We all squeezed as much of the water we could out of the sack, and heaved it into the hand cart we had brought along. We then pushed the cart to our apartment house, lugged the sack to the stairwell, placed it onto a board which we had left there, and somehow managed to slide it up the stairs to our attic rooms.

Papa had constructed a frame for some screening he had bartered a friend for, and for the next several days, we daily spread a layer of grain over the screen to dry out in the sunlight which came in through the skylight. After drying, it became my task to grind the grain in our small coffee mill. Mama then cooked some grits for us, using salted water in a vain attempt to disguise the taste of petroleum which had permeated the grain. She then tried adding some molasses, which still barely made the concoction palatable, as the molasses itself had also been contaminated before we had salvaged some from a bombed out warehouse. The main thing was, that it managed to fill our very empty stomachs.

Papa built Mama a *Kochkiste*, because fuel for the hearth was hard to come by. Also, electricity and gas supplies were erratic. Often, we barely had enough fuel to bring the pot of wheat grits to the boiling point. After bringing it to a boil, vegetables would be added, the pot would quickly be wrapped in a blanket and set into the cooking box, where it would simmer for hours until we sat down for our evening meal.

On June 1st, the Hamburger *Nachrichtenblatt*, a gratis news publication was put out by the Allied military regime. On July 14th, British Field Marshall Bernard Montgomery allowed his troops contact with the German population. Two weeks later, ten Hamburg movie houses were given permission to resume operations. The St. Pauli live *Plattdeutsches Theater*, which I joyously attended, gave a satirical, but humorous performance of the familiar Hamburg character *Zitronenjette*, in contemporary Allied occupation setting. Finally, the post office began to deliver mail, trolleys traversed the city, and ferries again criscrossed the Elbe. The harbor resumed its symphony of the sounds of labor.

"We cannot rebuild a destroyed city, nor make a democracy, on less than a daily 1500 calories." These were some of the words the SPD politician Max Brauer voiced.

On the 6th of August, 1945, Hamburg elementary schools were reopened. Of the 467 school buildings, 21% had been totally destroyed. 260 of the buildings still standing were under repair for governmental, hospital, and Allied forces use. Only 60 school houses, mostly at the edges of the city, were prepared for Hamburg's children. As of September 1st, 1657 teachers again continued their work with 80,852 students. The *Oberbau*, plus other vocational schools, began lessons only as of October 1st. 79% of male teachers, and 61% of females, were over age forty. Many pedagogues were still imprisoned, or, like Frl. Gertrude Schmidt, were being de-Nazified and working on rubble removal. I received written notification to resume classes at the Seilerstrasse. That meant, I either had to walk from the Nippoldstrasse to catch the large paddlewheeler *Harburger Dampfer,* or sprint in the opposite direction towards Wilhelmsburg to hop aboard the *Jollenführer* in order to steam through the bodies of water connected to the Elbe, and arrive at the *Landungsbrücken.* A brisk march would take me a good twenty minutes to reach the school on a clear day, but as Hamburg is known to have a rather wet climate, the saying goes that Hamburgers are born with an umbrella, and inclement weather usually caused me some delays. Needless to say, in the winter, the Elbe was occasionally frozen over, requiring icebreakers to clear a path ahead of the ferries. I was often late due to inclement weather, but also because, due to hunger, I lacked the stamina to keep up a brisk pace.

THE MAJOR ISSUES for the general population were food and shelter. Germany was the conquered nation. In the north, the Brits were the Allied forces in charge, and they made certain that all comestibles beyond the bare bone minimums required for the German population were routed to Britain. This policy resulted in the actual reduction of nutrition for Germans far beyond the deprivations suffered during the war.

I complained to my parents, "The war is over! I want to go back to America right away!" Mama then decided to see if the

American Consulate had returned. We still remembered how she had been chased by the Nazi guard when she inquired about the possibility of help for her American born children. Now, with the war finally over, the Allies were setting up embassies in Hamburg again. She had read that the Swiss Consulate was acting in the interim until the American Consulate staff arrived. I was so excited about this bit of information, that I could not sleep all night. The next morning, my mother, Erika, and I took the *Harburger Dampfer* to the *Landungsbrücken*, and from there to the heart of the city by trolley. We walked from the Alster to the Swiss Consulate. A tall, aristocratic, well-groomed, grey-haired lady ushered us into her office. She looked us over with great sympathy in her demeanor. After my mother had related our tale of having been stranded in Germany for the entire duration of the WWII, she inquired about the procedure of arranging passage back to the U.S.A.. With a clipped British accent, the Swiss lady said, "I will put your daughters on the list immediately. Then, I will try to notify your husband's brother Hans, so that he can provide for them until you and your husband can arrange for your visas to join them. At the moment, all visas are going to concentration camp victims." I was elated! However, my mother went into what I refer to as her Madonna and Child embrace with Erika. I knew then that she was highly reluctant to let my sister out of her sight, and that I would have to use all my powers of persuasion to sail home alone. Mama gave the Swiss consulate lady Uncle Hans' and Tante Grete's last known address, as well as other pertinent information. We then left the consulate to go to the Hamburg *Hauptpostamt* to register our name for any overseas mail coming in to be sent to our present address. The main post office was heated, and since it was damp and drizzly outside, we did not mind having to wait in line. I made a mental note of these cozy conditions, and later spent many an hour standing at one of the desks doing my school homework. Afterwards, I would lope down to the harbor to hop aboard a late boat home. When we left the post office, Mama, Erika, and I went into the basement of the *Alster Haus* department store to inquire as to the whereabouts of my friend Marion Meier, her brother, and her mother, who worked for the store. The store had converted its basement to living accommodations for war victims, and as Marion and her family had been rendered homeless due to the bombing, they had been given two bunk beds for their interim use. By chance, we met Marion coming out of the guard's office as we asked about them. She then took us to their two-bunk area in among dozens of double decker beds. "We are lucky to be located up against this wall," she said, "so that we have a little privacy in this corner." She then proceeded to take one of the blankets from a stack at the foot of the bottom bed, and draped it over the side of the beds, which gave us a small secluded space in which to visit. At a later date, those grey blankets were fashioned into winter coats for Marion and her mother. In my mind's eye, I still can picture them walking towards me on cold winter days snuggled in their blanket coats. Marion beckoned Erika and me to sit on the lower bunk, and pulled out a small chair from under a table for my mother. "Mutti arbeitet," she volunteered. Then she lamented, "If only we had our own place again!" We commiserated with her, and then I told her that I hoped to get back to New York where I was born as soon as possible. "Lucky you!" Marion replied in English.

We took the trolley through the devastated city, changed at the *Rathaus* to the one which would deposit us at the *Landungsbrücken*. The *Harburger Dampfer*, with its gangplank down and the crew poised for departure, quickly helped us aboard. We sat indoors, for it was chilly on deck. My mother talked about the events at the consulate. She explained that we did not know where Uncle Hans was, as we did not know if he had been detained as an illegal alien at some time during the war. As of the time when Papa had been deported, Uncle Hans' status had not yet been discovered.

Even before the concentration camp victims were to be permitted to leave, the American G.I.s were to be returned home. This however, required that the North Sea, the English Channel, and the North Atlantic had to be cleared of mines. German prisoners of war were pressed into the hazardous task of clearing the shipping lanes, this duty being performed with quite primitive equipment. How naive I was to believe that good times would begin to roll immediately following the cessation of hostilities.

All this was then discussed with my father, as we sat down to eat our wheat grits. Papa was thinking out loud, as he so often did, whether he could build on the Altona property. Mama laughed, then brought up the matter of the red tape we would encounter in applying for building permits. When she and I trudged to X number of city offices, the bureaucratic answers were always the same. "*Unmöglich!*" It was deemed impossible to rebuild on our property in light of the plans to completely alter the city street layout. Papa then decided to go ahead with his alternate plan to buy, lease, or rent a piece of property near the housing block. Besides having a place for us to live, Papa sorely missed having his own workshop. He had inherited his incredible pioneer spirit from his Prussian ancestors. "*Wo ein Wille ist, ist auch ein Weg!*" was his favorite proverb. (Where there's a will, there's a way!)

On the way to Wilhelmsburg, along the fence of the Free Harbor, were several *Schrebergärten.* These were small plots, similar to our American victory gardens, beautifully maintained by enthusiastic gardeners. Each piece of property had a wire, picket, or bush fence delineating the extent of each of the owner's boundaries. He found one site, approximately 15 x 25 meters in size, which noone else wanted because of a deep bomb crater which distressed most of the property. The crater extended partially under the high Free Harbor fence which bordered the back end of the lot. The fence had been badly twisted, leaving a deep gap under it. This hole provided a convenient alternate exit and short cut for the workers who would normally have to use the regular Free Harbor controlled gates, which were located almost a kilometer further down the road. How my parents, and with what barter they acquired the *Schrebergarten* lot, I do not know. But, one day soon after our registration at the Swiss consulate, Papa came home with papers for a 99 year lease of the land. He immediately began surveying, planning, and preparing the building site. While he was digging the trench for the footing of the cottage, Erika and I had to scrape and clean at least 25 bricks a day which were free for the taking at a designated bombed-out area in the neighborhood. We had to haul and deposit them on the lot for use as footing and foundation. Not having a son, my father recruited me as his helper, but, I must admit, a most unwilling candidate. Papa's determination to build us our own house was boundless. Of course, he needed more tools, materials, and a labor force. The Dutch and French prisoners of war whom he had befriended previously when we lived at the Altona apartment house, had either died in the bombings, or if had survived, had returned to their homelands. Now our family had to pull together more than ever.

My most important chore was to station myself on the submarine base bunker rooftop, guarding a pile of used lumber, doors, and window frames which Papa had previously gotten permission to dismantle for his project. He had scrounged a handcart, and he, Erika, now nine years old, and I would transport to the bomb crater lot. The inaccurate, but often efficient rumor mill made the best government information network seem ineffective. We were helped at odd times by some of the merchant seamen who came from all corners of the earth to unload cargo for the occupation forces. They would just physically push our cart, or come by to chat with my father to ask what he might need. Papa, as an exmerchant seaman, trusted most sailors. So, I and my mother were introduced to some of his new found friends. That is how I later met Jack. He was an officer on one of the British supply ships. His family had come from Russian aristocracy who had escaped to London after the 1917 revolution. Jack was in his early 20s, tall, slender, and handsome, but what was most important to me , had been to New York, and at least knew a great deal about the city. He could sing some of the latest hit songs, and told me about the bobby sock craze. We soon became good friends. However, we could only see each other briefly, for he had his onboard duties, and then would have to steam off for England with cargo. Between building projects, I commuted to classes at the Seilerstrasse, while Erika walked to the Wilhelmsburg elementary school. My enthusiasm for learning was diminishing for lack of energy due to poor nutrition. The building project became my father's main concern, and my help was needed more and more. Mama and Frau Winkler, in the meantime, traveled overland with whatever articles of value they could scrape together to barter for food. They sacrificed their last jewelry, cigarettes, or some of the blue and white checkered sheets I had recovered from the sub base, to trade for potatoes, carrots, or a piece of bacon. The farmers, however, had become so swamped with city folk seeking food, that they had grown annoyed and jaded with such items, and brusquely slammed their doors shut, unless particularly attracted by an unusual artifact. The British occupation forces then forbade the population to go *hamstern*, as it was called, and would confiscate all such barter items indiscriminately, to be then sent on to England. Mama lamented that autumn on how impossible the situation had become. Papa then decided to try a different tack, and I was taken along. Jack had given me some American cigarettes for my father, so we took those along to trade. We had taken a short ferry ride to *Altenwärder*, hoping to either be lucky to find a farmer who would appreciate American cigarettes, needed help in picking his apple crop, or needed broken machinery repaired. At each door, we were turned away. Finally, as we walked through the last long orchard to reach the farmhouse, and back again to the *chaussee*, Papa had had enough. "Helen, you keep watch; I'm going to pick up the *Fallobst!*" He opened his duffle bag and busily scooped up the windfall apples from the ground. I heard a door slam, and saw a man come out of the house carrying a shotgun. I shouted a warning to my father, and we both began to run down the street with the farmer and his dog in pursuit. Papa and I reached the ferry station in time to hop aboard and escape our followers.

As we arrived at *Neuhof*, we encountered a random Redcap British patrol commodities search in progress. With great apprehension, we approached the checkpoint. To our surprise, the officer in charge recognized my father, and called out to him, "Hello mate, did you and your daughter do some repairs on the farms?" "We tried," Papa answered. The Tommy cheerfully waved us through, and called after us, "Take your tools, and continue work on your land."

AT SCHOOL, I eagerly looked for my old class chums. Marion had been discovered at the *Alster Haus*, because we had remembered her mom's employment there. She had reported to me that Elfriede now lived in their *Poppenbüttel Schrebergarten* home, therefor, out of our school district. I already knew that Ursula's mother had died of tuberculosis, and Ursula was coping with the household and her little brother at the Deichstrasse. Marion and I both lamented how difficult it must be for her. Just then, we were delighted to find that she was once again one of our classmates. Her dark eyes were now even sadder, her slim body dangerously anorexic due to lack of food. Her father did not know how to stretch the now less than 1500 daily calory allotment the Allied government's ration cards supplied. The stores were empty, some bakers augmented the breads with sawdust or other dangerous fillers, making many sick. The investigations of these misdeeds were slow, for the horrors of the Nazi concentration camps had come to light in graphic detail. On *Anschlag Säulen* (poster columns), through newspapers and films, we were all appalled by the extent of the Nazi's bestiality, and shocked by what was revealed. I went to the Principal of our school to see if he could supply any direction as to information sources to find my Jewish godmother Hildegard Witt. He regretted that he did not know which bureaucracy was in charge of such details. Herr Rektor Bauer had gathered us in the auditorium, lecturing us on how difficult our lives are after the betrayal of such a Führer. A leader who coerced all of us, bringing an entire nation, including this once beautiful city to this sorry state. "You girls have been deprived of much. Chew your food slowly to extract every bit of nutrition out of every mouthful."

Day after day, I spent commuting by ferry through fog, drizzle, rain, snow, and wind. The cold was the worst element for me. The school, as well as many other public places, was not heated. Places such as the Reeperbahn cafes, theaters, dance halls, and the post office, that were heated, gave Marion and me welcome shelter. In the cafes, we ordered *Glühwein* (hot, artificial tasting coolaid type drinks) while doing our school homework. We hovered around the grates of the underground portions of the city transit system to absorb the heat radiating through our shivering bodies while practicing our English vocabulary, or reciting Goethe poems. "I'm going to be out of here as soon as possible!" I would repeat every day. "New York, New York," I chanted long before I knew of the popular song. Marion too, was affected by this lament. "Do you think that I'm going to stay in Germany when you are off to America? You just wait and see." Sure enough, years later, when I was married and living in Connecticut, running our own business called Dutch Village, at an old former stage coach station between New York and Boston, Marion showed up at our doorstep. She had married an RAF pilot, and was living in England and working for British Airways.

That November of 1945, Marion and I decided to find jobs as extras for the Christmas musical pageant at the Trichter theater. We had read the audition notices, and Marion prodded me to apply. We discussed the possibilities at great length with some artistic *Gymnasium* boys with whom we often exchanged homework help in one of the cafes. The proprietors did not seem to object to us hanging around, for we all scattered well before the adult crowd arrived. I was tempted to audition for a dramatic role, but Marion and the boys felt that I would be better suited to be among the dancers. After much palaver, I did decided that my extra time and energy had to be continued to be applied to helping my father with his building project. None of us wound up going to the audition, after all, but Ursula and I received tickets from our fathers to the first Christmas show to be performed after the end of the war. It was a lovely event, as well as a great diversion for us. We became regular operetta buffs, attending each new production until after *der Juxbaron,* when I left for the U.S.A.. That Christmas was the worst we as a family experienced. We had absolutely nothing to celebrate with; no food, no decorations, no music, and no heat. But, we were hugely thankful that the war at least was over. I remember looking at the Green Michael on my way home from the *Oberbau* during the holiday week, smiling to myself, "We have peace, that's all that counts!" Of course, Papa again coaxed me to help with his project. By now, the cottage had been framed and closed in. It had a front door leading into a hall, on one side of which was to be a kitchen/ family room, on the other, a future living room, which now housed all his tools, a work bench, and all materials not yet processed. He had left much of the bomb crater extend under the house to be used as a crawl space. It was stuffed with odd pieces of wood, beams, and planks which were to be used for the stairway to the second story. At present, we had to climb a ladder to get upstairs to our future bedrooms. One day, as I was again engaged in my usual task of straightening out Papa's workbench and tools, I was given the additional assignment of locating his set of false teeth, which he had taken out and misplaced somewhere among the clutter. They were very ill fitting, and caused him much discomfort. "I couldn't think straight with that damned plate in my mouth!" he lamented. Sure enough, I found the teeth in one of his tool boxes buried under some screw drivers. He was relieved to have them again, although he only reluctantly popped them back into his mouth. I was appalled. "They have to be washed first; they are probably crawling with bacteria." He just laughed, "Nothing with germs to live on have touched them in a week."

As we walked back to the housing block, we encountered the former Gestapo man. He was still dressed in black, although without insignia, his police dog along side of him. Incredibly, he was still in charge of the entire local constabulary. We knew that curfew was nearing, so we hurried past him without saying a word. *"Mach' schnell!"* He shouted menacingly, "One of these days you'll be late for the curfew." A few days after that, I was reminded of that threat. During a visit to our local woman physician to see if she could relieve me of a terrible rash I had on my hands and between my fingers. The piece of good, hard soap that I had received from my foster mother Frau Huber had been used up, and we all were reduced to using the horrible grey, gritty bars which were the only kind available with our ration cards. We later found out that these soaps had been made using the bones of concentration camp victims. As I sat in the doctor's waiting room, a well built, tall, blond and blue eyed young man asked me what my problem was. I showed him my hands.

"Oh, that's nothing. I'm sure Frau Doktor will be able to help you."

"Well," I said to him, "You look healthy enough to me. What's wrong with you?" As we were the only ones in the waiting room at the time, he proceeded to remove his jacket and shirt, revealing the S.S. tattoo on his arm. I gasped.

"Jah, those bandits branded me three months before the end of the war," he lamented. "I'm certainly not going to go through life with that on my body. By the way, the head of the Gestapo here on the Neuhof is still in charge, working with the local police to keep order for the British occupation forces," Helmut volunteered.

Frau Doktor came out into the waiting room to usher me into the examining area. I showed her my hands. "I'm sad to say that I have no medications to give you, nor does the apothecary." She confirmed that the horrible soap most probably had brought on the condition. "Try to buy some good, hard soap through the black market, or get yourself a boyfriend from the occupation force who can supply you. However, the British are still suffering from lack of food and commodities as much as we are, so look for an American merchant seaman, preferably a quartermaster," she said half in jest, but with a serious demeanor. "Here are a pair of cotton gloves. The next time you are working on the pile of rubble cleaning bricks, wear these. They may help a little."

As I left the office, Helmut called after me, "Can I come by to take you for a walk sometime, or don't us German boys have a chance any more?"

PAPA HAD SOMEHOW managed to get us a cooking stove for the kitchen in the cottage. "The most important things in life are home and hearth; everything will then fall into place," he said one day. This comment was uttered one morning after a most harrowing night of a battle with the largest rat I had ever seen. The two traps that Papa had brought back from the submarine base had been set up numerous times with pieces of cheese, or tiny pieces of seared bacon all of us would have rather eaten ourselves. But, Erika and I had had many sleepless nights screaming our parents awake when the rodents awakened us by leaping on our beds from the open eaves of our attic apartment. This particular night, Papa had to clobber the beast with a hatchet, because the animal was so large, that only its snout had been caught by the trap, and it was running around the room in panic. "That's it, girls, the biggest one is dead," Papa proclaimed, the hatchet still in his hand. The rats were so brazen, acrobatic, and invasive that they were active even during daylight hours. They came in all sizes and colors, black, brown, and grey, and were both long and short haired. "They are the largest of the gnawing family of rodents," Papa said, "in the same family as the house mouse. Just look at the size of this one!" He tried to make light of the incident. "This is perhaps the leader of the rat circus, or the gym instructor training the young." Papa laughed. "Helen, do you now see why I'm so anxious to get us into our cottage?" "Yes," Mama chimed in, "the girls know that. They also know that the female house rat can have up to twelve litters in one year, and up to twenty in a single litter." She went further into her dissertation on how harmful the creatures are to mankind, and all the horrible diseases they carry. She, who had been trained as a young woman in the Altona *Doktor Pilski Frauen Klinik,* was keenly aware of rats being a very serous threat to our health. This latest incident brought on a frenzied continuation of activity to get our cottage prepared for us to move out of the rat infested apartment.

However, another event made the situation even more urgent. The apartment had been an emergency quick fix construction, made available to us by the Howaldt shipyard to permit my father to be closer to his place of work. Now that the war was over, this priority no longer existed, and we were free to choose our own place of residence. Besides the rats, the tenant who had to share the mid-landing toilet with us constantly made our life further uncomfortable by playing cruel tricks on us. We had a large, old fashioned key used to unlock the toilet hanging in our hallway. The toilet was located one half flight below our attic apartment, and one half landing above the other tenant's flat. He was a mean, morose, and ill-tempered man, and I was afraid of him. Unlike my sister, however, who was of a rather fearful disposition, I never let anyone see that I was afraid. One day, I followed my usual practice of leaving the toilet key in the toilet door lock so that anyone could see that it was occupied, neglecting to follow my mother's advice to take the key inside with me, and hanging it on the door latch. I heard heavy footsteps on the terra cotta landing approaching the toilet, then heard the key being turned in the lock, and being removed. I called out that it was *besetzt,* and that I would be out in a minute. There was no response and I found myself locked in. I called out loudly in vain for more than half an hour, until my father, who had begun to worry, came down to see what had become of me. He had suspected some kind of trouble, and coming out into the hall, had heard my cries for help. Papa assured me that he would return immediately with a tool to spring the lock. After releasing me, he stormed to the apartment door of the tenant. I watched as the door opened. Without hesitation, my father accused the man of being a repulsive scoundrel, and struck him solidly twice on his cheeks. The fellow was toppled to the floor, with the most astonished expression on his face. The following day, Mama happened to have an appointment with the doctor. The culprit was sitting in the waiting room nursing a black eye, and glared at my mother hatefully, but silently. After examining my mother, Frau Doktor remarked, "It seems that your husband was responsible for giving the man that shiner. Congratulations! I'm sure he deserved it."

AFTER THE NEW YEAR, I became depressed. I had visited the Swiss consulate hoping that my paper work to leave Germany would be in process, but nothing had moved forward. The environment discouraged my dreams, hunger sapped my enthusiasm and physical strength, and listlessness descended upon me. It took all my willpower to commute to Oberbau classes. I found myself falling asleep during math and even my favorite literature lessons. Only my friends Marion and now Tamara, whom I had recently found again, managed to perk me up. I knew that I had to get out of Germany as soon as possible to retain my well being. I became determined to prepare myself for life back home in America by acquiring some useful skills, and also not to become emotionally involved with any of the boys or young men who were showing interest in me.

Tamara and her Russian mother both spoke with thick accents. They had determined not to live in a totalitarian environment again, and believed that life would be far better in Germany than in Russia in the future. I felt ashamed to have complained, since she and her mother were still living among the rubble. They had managed to clear a small section of the cellar of the house which they had previously occupied. Tamara's father had been on the Ukraine fighting front, and they knew nothing of his whereabouts, if he was still alive, or worse, held by the Russians in Siberia as a prisoner of war. The husband of one of Mama's Pinneberg relatives had been captured by the Russians, and sent to Siberia. Physically unfit for labor, he was released along with other seriously afflicted German prisoners, and sent home. He was so ill, that his comrades continually had to coax him to hang on until reaching Hamburg, and where he could at least die in his wife's arms. His wife and his two young daughters were waiting at the Altona *Hauptbahnhof*, but the train arrived with several hundred sick and crippled men, and one dead one.

Then there was my classmate Brigitte. She and her sister were the only survivors who had lived on their family estate, which had been originally deeded to them by Frederick the Great, the king of Prussia. Brigitte had been hidden by the remaining male servants when the Russians marched through. Her parents had perished when the soldiers set fire to the manor and the stables, and confiscated the horses. We all felt that she may not have escaped being raped, for she never spoke of her ordeal, but just attended class quietly.

Our family goal was to get out of the apartment during the January thaw. Then we would celebrate my 16th birthday, including Marion and Elfriede to the event. Erika was grinding batches of the wheat kernels we had rescued from the Elbe, and which my parents had been drying in the sun while trying to keep the rats at bay. Papa had scrounged metal boxes to store the dried grain in. It was a never ending battle to keep one step ahead of the rats. They could easily gnaw through wood and plaster, and even learned to push jars off shelves to scavenge the contents among the shards of glass, dining at their leisure. When they heard us coming, they would scurry to the roof beams, peek out from their hiding places, and wait for the next opportunity to try another tactic.

Mama and I did one more wash while living at the housing block. There were only two locations for running water to be used for purposes of washing. Of course, only cold water was available to soak our clothes in. First, we did the white things, then, in the same water, the colored clothes. We bent over our small tub which we stood on the sidewalk, rubbing on the washboard. We poured the dirty water into the street drain. Soap powder was often a luxury unavailable to us. In the summer, we hung the wash on long lines in the *Hof* (backyard), but we had to remain close by to assure that our clothes would not be stolen. In the winter, after we had dragged the heavy, wet wash up the four flights, Papa would further wring the towels and sheets, so they would not drip on the floor. No dry cleaner was as yet in business, so our winter coats, woolens, and navy slacks were worn until springtime. At Neuhof, we could be easily identified, for most of us had winter garments liberated from the German navy supplies, which were turtleneck sweaters, bellbottom trousers, and pea jackets. Papa had given me some of his regulation navy attire, which I had altered to fit me. I was fortunate to have a dark blue ladies' coat, so I looked quite fashionable wearing the sweater and slacks in a complete ensemble. My mother had given me some red wool yarn, which I used to embroider my initials HHB on the side of the sweater. Then, I trimmed the watch cap with red, and added a pompom. For the spring, that is, for Easter, almost every Neuhof female had a blue and white checkered outfit in various designs made from the *Kriegsmarine* bed sheets.

We moved our table, six chairs, two chests of drawers, five beds, and a kitchen cabinet piecemeal to the cottage on a handcart. Everyone on the peninsula now knew that we were moving. We still did not have the staircase installed, and had to use the ladder to reach the second floor. To bring the furniture upstairs, Papa had to rig a pulley system from a beam to have access through a window. The nickel-trimmed hearth was connected to the chimney in the kitchen. Mama was pleased that it worked well for cooking in addition to keeping us warm. Our kitchen/ family room was the only one heated. All activities, except for sleeping, were conducted here. Erika and I again shared one of the bedrooms, and our parents, the other. It always seemed to take me hours to fall asleep due to my cold feet, but thanks to my father's efforts, no rats were present. We celebrated the Sunday closest to my birthday by inviting Elfriede and Marion, who came by the *Harburger Dampfer* to be with us that afternoon for kaffeeklatsch, with ersatz coffee and the first cake to be baked in the new coal oven. For days, Erika had been grinding the wheat kernels again and again in the coffee mill, to as fine a flour as possible. My mother had bartered some of the petroleum molasses for eggs, to have for the cake. Part of another blue and white checkered sheet was used to sew kitchen curtains and the rest for a table cloth. We always kept four of our straight wooden chairs in the family room, and the other two in the bedrooms. Now, we brought them down for the celebration. Papa had whitewashed the kitchen, and had even found several Delft tiles for decoration around the stove. A single army bed was set against the wall to serve as a sofa, covered with *Kriegsmarine* blankets and plumped up pillows covered in, you guessed it, blue and white check. Next to the cupboard, which housed our dishes and pots, stood a bench supporting a pail and dish bowl which constituted our sink area. Our latest acquisition was a large milk can with handles on either side, which we carried out to the curb to be filled with water by the scheduled delivery truck. It was a blessing now no longer to have to drag water up four flights of stairs. Mama had gotten the can plus a steel ladle for translating several love letters to German girls from their British boyfriends. We gathered around the table eyeing my birthday cake, which looked to me like a cross between an Indian pudding and a southern cornbread. It tasted just great. Elfriede gave me a box with air holes on its sides and with soft meowing sounds emanating from it. When I opened the box, I discovered a young cat which was the spitting image of Mushi, the kitten I had owned in Bethpage, Long Island as a youngster, and kept clothed in doll dresses and a bonnet. This one was a frisky feline with perfect tiger stripes, white paws and bib. I was delighted with my gift, but what to feed this little creature? Elfriede read my thoughts. "She will be a perfect hunter, catching her own field mice!" She remarked. "Don't worry, the mother was an outdoor cat, and taught her well." We all sat down to enjoy the cake, which all thought was wonderful, but I still tasted the petroleum from the molasses. Marion threw a little package in my lap, and winked at me. I carefully unwrapped an enameled American flag pin. "That will look great on your navy blue coat," Marion said. Then they all sang Happy Birthday to me. It was really touching to share this celebration with them. Mama gave Elfriede a jar of the molasses for her parents, and a piece of the cake to Marion for her brother and mother. Elfriede and her family, which also included her grandparents, now lived comfortably on their former *Schrebergarten* land in Poppenbüttel. When the party was over, we made plans for our next visit. As Elfriede went to a different school, and we had no telephones and mail delivery was still sporadic, we always had to prearrange our gettogethers. I was to visit her and her family on the Sunday following the beginning of spring.

I walked my friends to the boat landing, and waved goodby to them with the pretty hanky with a blue border Erika had patiently crocheted around the edges. On my way back, before I reached the housing block, I strolled to my favorite little beach. I remember asking myself who the man was who was walking along the sand on *my* beach. He gazed across the water, half in reverie, but consciously aware of his reality. The man turned towards the shore, and seeing me, seemed to recognize me. He waved to me. I waited until his features were clear to me, and saw that it was Helmut, the young soldier I had met in the doctor's office. He ran towards me with a big smile on his face. "Saw you walking with your girlfriends," he said. "I was hoping to catch you alone. This is *my* favorite place, too, you know." Now I became embarrassed. I turned to leave the shore. "How are your hands?" He asked, before I could walk away. I was wearing the mittens that I had knitted with the help of Ria, back in my carefree days at York. He pulled off one of them and inspected the design. "Why, look at this! It's a bird." Then he grabbed my other, still covered hand, and inspected the intricate pattern. "My, the two make a perfect love bird pattern!" With that, he gave me a hug and my first kiss. Slowly, we walked hand in hand past the cottage of a fisherman and his wife whom I knew to chat with about the weather and their fishing cutter. She was the lady who had given me an eel wrapped in newspaper. The smoke rising from their chimney reminded me how fortunate they were to have both heat and the luxury of the food their fishing enterprise provided for them. There was still some snow visible in the gardens across from the housing block. As we walked along the sidewalk, we passed Frau Winkler's son, a known black marketeer, dressed in a dark coat with a white silk scarf draped over his shoulders, and conspicuous with his duck tail style black hair. He was chatting with Günther Morgenrot, who was later to marry my friend Irmgard. Helmut and I then knew that our stroll would soon be the gossip of the neighborhood. At the gate of my house, he again hugged and kissed me. My mother had just been looking out of the kitchen window, and opened the door to call out to me, "Bring your friend in for a piece of your birthday cake." Helmut was delighted to be invited into our kitchen. While she poured the *Muggefugge,* the local name for ersatz coffee, Mama asked him about his plans for his future. "I'm working to get my seaman's papers, and hope to become mate, and perhaps captain of my own vessel," he bragged, hoping to impress my father, who was resting on the daybed/ sofa. Erika was sitting at his side doing her homework. Papa then sat up and asked for a cup of coffee as well. The men then went on at great length about the dismal situation, cursing the Hitler regime each in their own way. Papa compared us all to just pawns on a chess board. Helmut lamented that he had been singled out by that Gestapo *Kerl* to be branded just three months before war's end. His broad smile was long gone, vanished behind a serious facade. "I'd better get home before curfew; that black clothed devil and his dog are just looking for an excuse to pounce on me any chance they can get," Helmut said. "Why is he still in authority?" Papa asked. "You don't know why?" Helmut was astonished that Papa did not know, but then he continued, "That's right, you were all still in America during our great depression and inflation." Papa laughed bitterly. "We had a great depression in the U.S., too. Many immigrants from different nations left to return to their home countries in the hope of finding better times. That had never happened before." Helmut then said that his father had told him that all of Neuhof and surroundings had been predominantly communist. It seems that the Gestapo man was, at that time, a big wig in the red party. Then, when Hitler came to power, he immediately switched to the NSDAP, and was promoted to persuade all his former comrades to defect and join the Nazis. Since he also was a labor boss, he was in a position to hire only those workers who agreed to convert. We were amazed at this story, but we still could not understand why the man was not placed into the denazification program. Helmut now laughed bitterly, "The Russians, who are part of the allied occupation forces, put political pressure on the British to reward any former communists, and the Brits felt obligated to appease them." After thanking my mother for the refreshments, Helmut kidded me for not obtaining real coffee from my British merchant seaman friend. I pushed him out the door, and called out after him, "Hurry up, and don't get caught out after curfew!"

"Well," my parents commented, "you certainly had an eventful sixteenth birthday!"

IT WAS COLD and nasty the next day. I walked towards Wilhelmsburg to catch the *Jollenführer* to the Landungsbrücken. My parents had given me a municipal travel pass which was valid on all Hamburg ferries and trolley cars. From the waterfront, I hopped on to the Reeperbahn trolley to reach my school. They had also given me pocket money to spend on *Glühwein*. Previously, I had always sprinted or loped to school to save my money in order to have it to spend at the local café hangouts. I arrived at school late that day, because the trolley schedule was irregular. I politely knocked on the classroom door, and Herr Fliege bade me enter. He was our English teacher, and always wore a bow tie, so he was nicknamed "Fliege" (fly) by the students. If I recall, his real name was Schultz. He remarked on how fashionable I looked, and when he spotted my new American lapel pin, commented, "I'm sure that you are very well prepared for this morning's English vocabulary test!" Of course, I was not, but I vowed to spend more time studying the more sophisticated English being used in his studies of literature, such as Shakespeare and Milton.

After school, I hung out with Marion, Tamara, Hannelore, whom I knew from the Weihe children's camp, and a short, cute girl I called *Mäuschen*, who sometimes tagged along when we were in a group. She was of a happy disposition, smiling more often than all of us combined. *Mäuschen* often made me laugh. I would catch her looking at me when I gave my long speeches on whatever topic turned up. I would stand up at the table for effect, then asked for help with my algebra homework as a reward for my entertainment. "Helen *hält Hof* (holds court)!" We all had many complaints about the current state of affairs. I remember asking her about her thoughts on why our school system had taken care of our well being as required by the Hamburg Hanseatic school system, even during the previous regime, but now, under the Allied forces, we were given no lunch or milk, and our teachers were so depressed that they were not able to function to the best of their abilities. A few weeks before our Principal handed us our final, but rather incomplete diplomas, he apologized for the lack of his as well as the teacher's lackluster efforts, attributing them to hunger and deprivation we were all suffering from in this grey, rubble pile of a city. When *Mäuschen* asked me what I intended doing in the near future, I again lamented that my paperwork to return to the U.S. was still in limbo. I had heard that the German prisoners of war were still busy clearing the shipping lanes of mines, and noone could predict how long that process would still take.

One day, I received word from my former teacher, Frl. Gertrud Schmidt, inviting me per letter to a concert in Hamburg. She had finally been "de-Nazified" after months of grueling physical labor clearing rubble. She was now teaching somewhere in a makeshift school. Before the concert began, while we waited for the orchestra to tune up, she urged me to pick up my violin again. I told her of the months of work, I, too, had spent in the rubble clearing bricks for my father to process for the building of our cottage. Also, the long hours I had spent guarding the pile of dismantled window frames, doors, etc.. I took off the blue lace gloves my friend Anna had given me a lifetime ago. Frl. Schmidt gasped, "What happened to your beautiful hands?" I answered, "Oh, they're finally healing after I used the good American soap I traded for my Navaho Indian ring at the Free Harbor black market. "The fellow was a swarthy chap, who was chatting me up!" I remembered telling my teacher, falling into the British cadence when I conversed with her. "Your conversational English was always good. Did Herr Schultz introduce you to Shakespeare and Milton yet?" she asked. I told her that his lessons had been uninspiring, but that I had learned to appreciate Shakespeare by reading him in modern German. I did confide to her that my favorite school day was when we met in the Speckstrasse, next to the house that Johannes Brahms had lived in, for our cooking classes, as this was the only school location that had kitchen facilities. Our teacher there was quite nearsighted, and wore thick glasses. We all had to cover our hair with babushkas while we stood in front of the stoves, which were either electric, gas, or coal burning. We usually sat on stools along tables three meters in length. There were only three tables, accommodating eight stools each. At each table, we prepared a different dish. At each gathering, we would use a different stove to cook on in order to gain experience with the various types of equipment. Each table unit prepared their assigned dish, and one student was to bring the pot to the stove in use, and stay with it to watch and stir. My group always picked me for this duty, in order not to spoil the dish, for the girls were extremely anxious not to ruin them, and they seemed to have more confidence in my abilities than their own. When other girls were called upon to perform various duties, they pushed me ahead to take their places, and, because the short sightedness of the teacher made it difficult for her to distinguish individuals, we always managed to get away with this tactic. Since we always got to eat whatever we had prepared, the fare was an important addition to our meager diets. During one of the early lessons, we made a vegetable soup containing mostly turnips. The teacher gave the second group a package of Kneckebrot to share with the thin soup. For dessert, the third group chopped up a few apples to be baked with just a little cinnamon sprinkled over them. We all were happy to enjoy the fruits of our labors.

Frl. Schmidt and I both enjoyed the concert, which consisted of excerpts from Scheherazade and some Brahms pieces. During intermission, she kept urging me to think about my future, "Prepare yourself to become a professional. You have a whole lifetime ahead of you. Don't get involved with any man you are incompatible with." She always gave me as many lectures and admonitions as my parents did, whom she admired very much. She told me that they were of the kind of pioneering stock that had made the U.S. great, and were a symbol of courage for her here in dismal Germany. We, as always, shook hands when we parted, for the North Germans are a reserved lot.

THE SUNDAY AFTER the first day of spring, as previously planned, I made the ferry, trolley, and Stadtbahn trek to visit Elfriede and her family. It was wonderful to see her parents and grandparents so snug in their little ranch style house, which was surrounded by rows of carefully laid out future vegetable beds, and interspersed with berry bushes, and a few fruit trees. We reminisced about our musical sessions, and they, too, urged me to resume my violin practice. After an ersatz kaffeeklatsch, Elfriede played on the piano, and I realized how much I missed our musical get togethers. Then, as we parted, her mother gave me a date on the calendar when she would be taking Elfriede into the city. We planned to meet in one of the Reeperbahn cafés.

When I once again arrived on the peninsula, I strolled to my beach. It was early evening, and I remember walking onto the sand as if in a dream. I continued walking right into the river. All I would have to do is to allow myself to be swallowed up by the Elbe, and there would be peaceful oblivion. The icy cold element shocked me, and the image of my dead grandmother appeared before my eyes. I heard her voice say to me, *"Der Herr ist treu, Er bewahrt dich vor dem Argen!"* This admonition startled me back to reality. I schlepped myself out of the water. I thought about the famous To Be or Not To Be soliloquies from Hamlet, but the words came to me in German. The fisherman and his wife had been busy on their boat, but had evidently been watching me, and came running towards me. They assisted me into their cottage. The woman helped me take off my waterlogged blue coat, and I removed my muddy shoes and white socks. I stood in front of the kitchen hearth in my wet dress, shaking it to speed up the drying. All she said was, *"Mädchen, das tut man nicht!"* Once I had stopped shivering, and my coat had dried sufficiently, I put back on my socks and shoes. I realized that I should not have contemplated doing what I had started to do; she needn't have even scolded me. I thanked her, and walked solemnly back to our cottage. My mother had given me a key, which I kept, together with my wallet, in my coat pocket. I let myself in, hoping that my parents would be napping in their bedroom, but they had heard me. As I entered the kitchen where they were sitting, my mother immediately noticed my disheveled condition, and asked me suspiciously what had happened to me. "I slipped off the ferry gangplank, and fell into the water," is all I answered. Mama carefully hung my coat over the perennial clothesline above the stove. "Good thing you didn't have on your navy woolen bell bottoms, you would have been dragged under very quickly. Tsk, tsk, tsk, *nah, so was!*" she muttered to herself. Then, she stuffed my shoes with old rags to absorb the moisture and placed them under the hearth to dry.

A WEEK OR two before graduation, *Mäuschen* came up to me during recess, as I headed for the rest room. "I have something important to tell you!" she said with a serious demeanor. "Do you have time later today to come to my house, before you head to the Landungsbrücken?" "Of course," I answered immediately, for I had never seen her without her smile. "Good, you're coming home with me, and we'll all talk about it! You'll still have enough time to get home before curfew." I was on pins and needles for the remainder of the school day, and could hardly wait to tell Marion that we could not hang out together today. After class, *Mäuschen* was waiting for me in front of the school. We walked to a trolley which took us to the Alster Pöseldorf district. Now that I had a monthly commuting pass, I was able to fully enjoy the advantages of the extensive transportation system which crisscrossed the city, but it nevertheless still was a dismal experience in view of the ubiquitous shamble which once was considered the Venice of the North. I do not remember exactly where my little classmate lived, but it was in a once fashionable area of beautiful townhouses. She and her family were very fortunate to have managed to keep all of their worldly possessions, with only minor damage to their building. However, as in most other houses, only the parlor windows had been reglazed, as glass was still at a premium. We were ushered in by Mäuschen's mother, who was waiting for us with tea, zwieback, and homemade jam. The teapot was covered by a cozy in the same design as my grandmother's, and I was urged to help myself with the toast and marmalade, while she poured our tea. I had the feeling that I was on display, and being evaluated. Finally, when I felt that I had eaten and chatted enough, I said to her mother, "I appreciate your hospitality, and I can see how fortunate Mäuschen and you have been to have missed being bombed out." Just then, before I could make a move to depart, a door into an adjoining room opened, and a man entered. He was introduced to me as my friend's father. Herr Richter, which was not his name, but his professional title of judge, asked me to step into his office, and sit down on a leather chair opposite his large oak desk. He told me that his daughter had given him many reports about my "court" sessions in school and at the cafés, and that he was a judge in the Hamburg judicial system. "We need conscientious English speaking legal apprentices in our courts. I would like to recommend you to my attorney friend Heinrich Aschermann, who has an office *am Messberg*, if you are interested. His office would be within fairly easy commuting distance for you." Then he got up, shook hands with a, for once, speechless Helen, and handed me a reference note to his colleague.

All, or nothing at all

The trolley ride back from the heart of the once fashionable
district of Hamburg was a blur to me. I arrived in a happy and
dream-like state at the Landungsbrücken, and hopped on
board of the ready to depart *Jollenführer.* I was greeted by the jolly
ticket taker/ first mate with, "Who fell in love with you today?"
That brought me out of my reverie. "Noone in particular, only the
world!" I answered. We both laughed, and he became the first
person to be informed that I might get a law apprentice position.
"Keine Angst, das wird schon klappen!" He assured me. Of course
I was fearful that perhaps I would not qualify. I knew that I had
made a good impression on the judge, but his friend and colleague
was the one who would be hiring me after another interview. I
reached into my coat pocket for the paper, and read the address to
where I was to report the next day to the first mate. He gave me
directions as to which trolley I was to take from the
Landungdbrücken. On my way home from the Wilhelmsburg area,
I passed the field where Helmut had his soccer practice. He was
busy with his sport, but had one eye on the road, to spot me as I
passed. He came running towards me with the ball in hand, almost
out of breath. He managed to ask, "What are you so happy about?"
In true character of my nickname, I blabbed out my latest news.
"That's great, anything that will keep you here in Hamburg is
good!" Then he kissed me on the cheek, and ran off with his ball
back to the field.

My mother and Erika were working in front of the cottage.
They had laid out a garden. For many weeks they had been
building a compost heap with new mulch in a corner of the lot. The
soil on the property had been churned so badly from the bomb that

had struck the site, that it had brought the sandy subsoil to the surface. Both had labored diligently to smooth out the terrain, filling in the depressions with as much sand as possible, and depositing the precious dark soil on the top. Mama had planned out neat rows, with Papa executing the layout according to her instructions. Erika was Mama's garden helper, as I was Papa's construction apprentice. I was much relieved not to have to work in the agricultural end of our family maintenance, as I intensely disliked gardening. They looked up from their vegetable planting activities with eagerness. I stood there, just smiling. My mother was the first to speak, "ABC has already told the world," she said in German, but continued in English with, "Well, tell us the latest, American Broadcasting Company!" At first, I was going to withhold my description of the tea party event until dinner, but I was much too excited, so I put on a performance in the yard. Of course, I repeated the occasion elaborately at dinner, like a well rehearsed stage play, for the amusement of my father. Papa laughed, and Erika and my mother clapped, while I took bows. "What a lawyer she's going to make!" Papa then said, "Too bad, I had hoped that you would become a marine architect, designing layer cake, cream color steam ships. By the way, I was going to get you a job as an apprentice draftsman at the Howaldt shipyard." He believed that just because I loved to sketch dream ship ocean liners, I would enjoy learning to become a designer. Now I was even more relieved to have this law apprentice opportunity.

When my friends and schoolmates later heard of my good fortune, they all agreed that it was the ideal occupation for me. "You, with your gift of gab," Marion said, "are the perfect candidate." She then added, "When you get back to New York, you can get into politics."

Immediately after leaving *Mäuschen's* tea party, I had made a call from a public phone, to Herr Aschermann's office, and his secretary set up an appointment for me for the following day. *Mäuschen's* father had been right, for it was a convenient trolley ride along the waterfront, past the Deichstrasse area of the historic merchant houses, one of which we had occupied during the war, and, to this day, are a charming tourist attraction. The office building was relatively undamaged, except for the windows, which mostly remained covered with cardboard, wooden shutters, oilcloth, or black roofing paper. I came into a long room with book cases on either side. The secretary sat at a desk at the far end, with a single glazed window to her left side. I introduced myself, and she went into the next room. She promptly returned, and held the door open for me to enter Herr Aschermann's office. He sat behind a large, oak desk, and from in back of him, the room was illuminated by one freshly glazed window. Two other windows remained covered with plywood. Two leather chairs stood in front of the desk, and he motioned for me to sit down in one of them. *"So, Sie sind Fräulein Helen Blescus,"* emphasizing the *Fräulein.* "I was told that you were born in New York, and have the best English verbal ability in your class." "Well, I don't know if I have the best, but I try." Herr Aschermann answered, "That's what I need from you. As you can perhaps see, I tried to retire from law during the war, but now, with the Allied forces governing the city, I've been urged by the British to resume my practice." He then stood up and walked to one wall which was covered with long rows of case files. "Look, the glass shards, plaster, and dirt from the blown out windows are still between my dead files. Only the new client folders are on the clean shelf below. It has been almost a year since the end of the war, but all recovery takes time, especially after such a devastation as we all experienced. You and your parents lost your apartment house, and I hear that your father was pressed into the submarine repair service by the Nazis. Yes, we all have our tragedies from this terrible war," he said softly. Then he turned slowly to go back to his desk and sit down again. I noticed his skin begin to change from a leathery appearance to a jaundice pallor. "Are you all right, Herr Aschermann?" I asked. "Can I get you some water?"

"No, but thank you for your concern. My old war wounds act up now and then." He dismissed his discomfort, and pulled his chair over to the typewriter at the end of the desk. Putting in a form letter, he typed in my name, address, and position as law apprentice, to be assigned to his office. "Please take this to the *Arbeitsamt*, and bring it back to me with the official stamp on it. I would like you to start work with us as soon as you have graduated." He then got up, walked me to the door, and informed his secretary that I would be a new addition to the firm. We shook hands, and I was pleased that my hands had healed sufficiently for me not to have to wear my blue gloves any longer.

The following day, I decided to go to the *Arbeitsamt* first, before going to class. I was fortunate not to find a long line. I asked to have my work paper stamped, and informed the clerk that the position had been assured me. She, however, told me that I would have to graduate first and have my diploma in hand before she could approve my application. At first, I was annoyed about this bureaucratic behavior, but my mother later reminded me that a fiefdom of such proportions as a labor bureau does not give their stamps of approval without involving a good deal of red tape. "Go back next week with your graduation paper, and then they should have no further excuses to withhold the stamp of approval." I followed her suggestion after graduation, and this time flashed a happy smile at the *Frau Beamtin*. I pushed my diploma onto the counter, and requested that the work permit be stamped. "*Tut mir Leid*," she said arrogantly. "Sorry, but you cannot receive permission to work .Your dossier shows that you are an American citizen."

Stunned by this peremptory refusal, I sat down on a bench in the outside hall to collect my thoughts and plan my next step. I decided to go to the Swiss Consulate and tell the tall, aristocratic lady about my predicament. It was a lovely spring day, and I enjoyed the trolley ride to the Alster district. As luck would have it, she was not busy at the time, and her secretary ushered me into her office. I was greeted warmly, but when I told her of my predicament, she frowned, thought for a while, and gave me the same excuse I had received from the woman at the labor bureau.

Now I became despondent, but she offered one ray of hope with the announcement that the American Consulate would soon be opening its doors. She then got up, and guided me out of her office. Since I was near the *Alster Haus*, I dropped by to see Marion. She, also, was an excellent English student, and had been hired by the British as a translator. All her papers had been approved, as she was a German citizen.

My next stop was to Herr Aschermann's office. With outrage, I told him of my dilemma. "*Macht nichts!* It doesn't matter. We won't worry about that stamp of approval," he shrugged it off with a flick of his hand. "We'll see what your American Consul General says when the office opens." I was put to work immediately straightening out the dead files, and storing them on the highest shelf. As an afterthought, he said, "*Übrigens*, by the way, everything you see in this office is strictly confidential. You know what that means! Please do not discuss our cases with anyone."

I took this admonition very seriously, which did not come easily to me. In the following months, I became more and more aware of cases of atrocities and abuses committed by the Hitler regime, not only against the Jewish population, but also against the Gypsies, and many others of our neighborhood who had not been in compliance with the Nazis. When time permitted, I was able to browse through many of the professional publications and the daily *Hamburger Nachrichten* to help me to become better informed of the happenings affecting my duties in the office. Of particular interest to me, and a subject that I would be fascinated by for the rest of my life, was the question of how such an ambitious, devious, power hungry man of Austrian descent worked his way to a leadership position, and then drove an entire nation to ruin. How Adolf Hitler died was a major topic of discussion for many months, not only for the Germans, but for the entire world. Being now involved in the legal profession, I became interested in the Nuremberg trials, which lasted for four years. I shall never forget the comment by Hermann Göring: "Naturally, the common people don't want war; neither in Russia, nor England, nor, for that matter, in Germany. That is understood. But, after all, it is the leaders of the country who determine the policy, and it is always a simple matter to drag the people along, whether it is a democracy or a fascist dictatorship, or a parliament, or a communist dictatorship. Voice or no voice, the people can always be brought to the bidding of the leaders. That is easy. All you have to do is tell them they are being attacked, and denounce the peace makers for lack of patriotism, and exposing the country to danger. It works the same in any country."

FROM AN EARLY age, even before entering school in Bethpage, L.I., I had been a voracious reader, beginning by deciphering the backs of cereal boxes and canned goods labels, and neon signs and billboards on New York city streets. Of course, I felt that I had to be the best defender of America from the moment that I arrived in Germany. So the history of the U.S. was read through the idealistic eyes of a New York girl, who remembered her island birthplace through tales of Manhattan Indians, the Statue of Liberty, and the Empire State Building. Now those rose colored childhood tales featuring Hollywood films of the Wild West and Shirley Temple had been displaced by the reality of everyday life in a defeated country, surrounded by the law books of a Hanseatic Hamburg lawyer. Frl. Jensen answered the phone and typed up the reams of required paperwork which I then had to deliver to the vast bureaucratic maze in the *Rathaus*, *Gerichtsgebäude*, the prison cells beneath the court house, and the British military headquarters. I would often also have to go to several of the seemingly endless offices manned by *Beamte* (officials), who then stamped, or made copies of the documents I had delivered. They always needed a receipt, a copy, or the original to put into their files in addition to the ones I required to put back into my briefcase to be brought back to Herr Aschermann, and deposited into folders on the office shelves. I traveled every trolley line to various other administrative buildings, and became expert in dealing with the mostly obstructionist white collar workers infesting them. As far as I could see, they seldom added anything useful to Hamburg civil or legal society.

Many of Herr Aschermann's clients were business women, who could not deal with the often extremely shattered lives of former soldier husbands, and only saw divorce as a way to save their own sanities. The men who needed his services mostly had been caught in local raids of various locations that had been loosely set up as black markets. Several, however, were big time black marketeers. One such, a wheeler dealer with connections to the British occupation forces supply houses, was the big fish caught by both the Hamburg and the British military police. Herr Aschermann was the defending attorney. I was kept busy hurrying from one municipal office, police station, and British military headquarters, to collect and distribute the paperwork. Finally, after weeks of work and visits to the jail in the holding tank prison in the basement of the courthouse, I had a briefcase full of documentation ready for my employer to take to the important trial. He had taken the heavy attache case personally, and told me to meet him with another document which Frl. Jensen was still typing up, at the British headquarters building where the trial was going to be held. He had had an earlier court appointment at the Hamburg *Gerichtsgebäude* before meeting me. I arrived at the headquarters early, and was told by the two military guards to wait at a bench in the lobby until Herr Aschermann arrived. When I saw him walking up the stairs, I realized that he did not have the briefcase with him. I hurried towards him, and could see that he did not look well. I knew that he did not care to be reminded of any infirmities, so I did not inquire how he felt. He was much relieved to see that I had arrived early, and called out, "*Frl. Blescus, ich habe die Tasche verlegt!*" He was terribly agitated that he had misplaced the briefcase. A mental picture flashed before me, and I said, "Which men's room did you go into in order to recover?" He was astonished that I would ask that question, but answered, "I was on the second floor of the court house dealing with the previous case." I assisted him to the bench, and told the two guards that my employer was ill, and that I would return shortly with some papers vital to the upcoming trial. The soldiers called after me, "Take your time, Blondie, we'll keep an eye on your boss."

I was lucky not to have to wait long for a trolley, and hopped aboard one quickly. At the court house, I rushed up the two flights, for I hated to use the elevators, which I considered to be dangerous. They consisted of open boxes with no doors, continuously moving, and one had to be agile to step on board at just the right time. Once, due to ice on my shoes, I slipped as I was getting off one, and badly twisted my ankle. I knew exactly where every rest room in every government and most public buildings was located. The men's room Herr Aschermann had most likely used, I reasoned, had to be near the cloak room where he would have donned his black robe for the previous trial. There was a bench standing in a niche off the hall with an intact, beautiful, stained glass window behind it. I had noticed the white enameled plaque saying *Herren* (men's room) near the bench. It was a fairly dark corner, only illuminated by the diffused light coming from the stained glass window. Sure enough, next to the bench, near the wall, stood the briefcase. I grabbed it, ran down the stairs, and out of the building to hop onto another trolley returning to the British headquarters. I arrived in the nick of time to quickly hand the case to Herr Aschermann, who had in the meantime sufficiently recovered. Nonchalantly, he took it from me, while the two guards opened the double doors to usher him into the courtroom. I could see a panel of military officers sitting in readiness. I sat waiting in the entry hall on a marble bench, with the two Brits vying for my attention. They told me that a traveling circus and some rides had been set up *auf dem Heiligen Geistfeld*, and would I meet them at the fair grounds, and bring one of my girlfriends along on the coming Sunday afternoon.

As it happened, just days before this incident, while I had been knocking on various bureaucratic office doors, I also had to go to the *Rathaus*. That building was always my favorite, but I did not know which office I was supposed to find. So, I looked for the ladies' room first, then wandered aimlessly around the halls, having trouble finding the correct room number. At random, I knocked on one of the doors. I heard a man's voice call, "*Herein!*", and entered. The man sitting behind the desk looked up with astonishment, and said, "Helen, *unsere Amerikanerin!*" He got up and greeted me warmly. "We were all wondering if you and your family were alive after this horrible war. Irmgard will be so happy to know that you have survived." I was just as astonished to find Irmgard's father here as he was to see me. Tears streamed down his cheeks, which he quickly wiped away, feigning a cold. Herr Scheel told me that he and his wife Erna, my mother's close friend, and my friend Irmgard lived *auf Waltershof*, which was located across the water from Neuhof. It was the ferry stop before our peninsula via the *Harburger Dampfer*. *Waltershof* could also be reached daily from morning until curfew by means of an industrial ferry several times a day. I was so happy to hear that my friend was alive. Our first meeting had resulted in a fist fight, but had blossomed into a close friendship. Her father marveled at the law apprentice position I had achieved, and gave me directions to their home as well as to the office I had been searching for.

The following day, I went to visit Irmgard and her family, using the industrial ferry. I could not afford to stay too long at that time, so I made an appointment to meet her on the Sunday afternoon ferry, and we would spend time together at the fair. I was careful not to mention that I had promised to meet the two British soldiers in front of her parents, for I knew that they would disapprove.

On Sunday, I took the *Harburger Dampfer* from Neuhof. It was a lovely and mild May day, and I stood at the deck rail as the ferry approached *Waltershof*. As we docked, Irmgard boarded the vessel. She was even more of a chatterbox than I, and we only became aware of the time as we neared the *Landungsbrücken*. I then told her that the two soldiers, Tom and Harry, were to meet us at the fair. "You mean two of the English allied forces?" She inquired. "Yes," I answered. Then it dawned on me to ask her how her studies in English were, to which she replied in German, "*So wenig wie möglich* (as little as possible)." Then she added, "My father would not be too happy about this, if he knew. However, I'll tag along this one time." Our dates spotted us walking towards the fair. Both were tall, good looking chaps, one blond, and the other dark haired. It did not make any difference in my preference, since both had approached me with equal fervor. However, in light of the attitude of my friend, I decided to introduce her to the blond one as her escort. It turned out to be the most awkward double date I have ever been on. Irmgard's English vocabulary was almost nonexistent, even though it was required study in the Hamburg school system.

She had done little to maintain a second language, and the soldiers spoke absolutely no German. By the time she has mentally translated something one of the men had said, the conversation had gone well ahead of that topic, so she remained totally lost. Thank God, the weather was beautiful, and we had a lovely stroll past some park-like areas, which took our minds off the devastation of the city. We heard the hurdy-gurdy carnival music of a carousel. My escort helped me onto a beautifully carved wooden horse, and swung himself on behind me. Irmgard and her soldier sat in a fantasy coach. It was a romantic ride, however, I was looking for a way out because of Irmgard's awkwardness. It was taxing for me to carry on the translations for all three of them. The soldiers spotted an amusement house which had a blast of air coming up at the entrance. One of them stationed himself below the raised area with a camera to photograph our legs as we tried to negotiate a moving grate. Somewhere among Tom's or Harry's postwar photos, are most likely pictures of our legs. For Irmgard, that was the last straw. When the chaps tried to prod us to walk the gauntlet again, she ran off. This, of course, put a complete damper on our afternoon, and so I excused myself and went off after Irmgard. Once out of their sight, we strolled down to the *Landungsbrücken,* reminiscing about our childhoods. "Remember the show we put on in the back ballroom of my father's *Gastwirtschaft*?" Irmgard asked, and continued with, "You sang and danced in spite of the *Verbot!*"

"Yes, I remember." I sang the song to her:

> *Ich hab' ein Goldenes Kleid,*
> *Ein Federhut so breit-*
> *Zwei Handschuh' aus Glacé*
> *Ein leeres Portmonnae.*

Then, I sang the American song: The Merry-go-round Broke Down, as We Went Round and Round.

We both laughed and cried at the memory. "That was a long time ago," I said. "Will we ever laugh and dance like that again?" "It was the last time I saw my cousin Günther alive," Irmgard whispered. "Soon after that, he was drafted and trained to drive Panzers. He died on the Russian front." By this time we had boarded the *Harburger Dampfer*, and were quietly sitting on the afterdeck, staring at the wake of the vessel. Before disembarking at *Waltershof*, Irmgard said, "Let's meet near St. Pauli each Friday. I know a mother and son who teach ballroom dancing. I'll arrange it. Here's my grandmother's address. We'll meet there."

THE FOLLOWING MORNING, Herr Aschermann came out of his office when I called out, *"Guten Morgen!"* as I entered. He motioned to me to sit down across from his desk, and began to thank me for the good work I had been doing, in particular for finding the misplaced briefcase in time for the important trial at British headquarters. "I have taken the liberty of registering you at the Hamburg University for the study of law." I was delighted with this news. He continued praising me for my work, which would now be augmented by my upcoming studies. He also offered to pay for my commuter ticket, which coincidently equaled my pay as apprentice, and caused me to smile inwardly. I had been using the ticket, which my parents had paid for, for my travels for the office. Although the gesture was certainly welcome, the most important thing to me was the legal training I was receiving. My employer then remarked that he had heard that the American Consulate had reopened its doors. As soon as I had completed my errands that morning, I headed for the Swiss Consulate, for I did not know where the American office was to be found. I was again received warmly, and given the address of the American Consulate. I immediately went to the location. There, I was ushered into the Vice-Consul's office by a well dressed, heavily made up American secretary. An American soldier was leisurely draped over a reclining chair, with his legs sprawled onto the desk. When I entered, he retracted his legs slightly, barely enough to observe me, but remained in his comfortable position. He motioned to me, and said, "Have a seat, Blondie; what can I do for you?" For a moment, I did not know what to say. I felt as if I were on a Hollywood movie set. Then I told him my name, and that I had been to the Swiss Consulate previously, who were going to process my papers to get back to New York City, where I had been born. Now, he retracted his legs completely, stood up, and shook hands with me. "Hello, Helen of Manhattan, I have heard all about you," he said. Now, I was embarrassed. "What have you heard?" I asked. He returned to his former casual position, and remarked, "You are working for an attorney, I hear." "Yes," I replied, "but without working papers!" Then I went into a tirade about the chain of bureaucrats I had approached. I lamented that none of them were of practical survival value, but only obstructionist. Where was the freedom that I hoped would follow at the end of the war? "And another thing: some of the Nazi *Beamte* are still in their same jobs, in particular, the head of the police of Neuhof." The young Vice Consul just listened patiently, while I went on and on. Finally, I ran out of breath. He retracted his long legs, sat up straight in his office chair, and began with, "My dear child, you are wearing rosecolored glasses. An occupation force cannot permit chaos to prevail after an invasion. It takes time to find qualified people to begin to run the government under a democratic format, but until then, we are forced to use the only officials with experience, in this case, regretfully, the Nazis. In the meantime, we have to get the shipping lanes cleared of mines so that we can begin to send our soldiers home. I will make sure that you will be one of the first of the American citizens to get passage back." With that, he stood up, brought me to the door, and patted me on the shoulder, soothing me like a father would a hurt child.

I BELIEVE THAT I dropped by the *Alsterhaus* to tell Marion my latest news, but also to invite her to take ballroom dance lessons with Irmgard and me. She declined the lessons, but said that she would be able to secure some invitations to special events after we had graduated from the dance program. For the next six Fridays, Irmgard and I met for our dance lessons in the St. Pauli dance studio. She had given me the address of her grandmother's small flat, which was just a few blocks from the dance studio. I came there to meet her after work. That meant that each Friday, I would not have anything to eat after my morning breakfast of grits, until I got home on the last ferry before curfew. Nobody that I knew really ever had enough food to share. Once in a great while, perhaps, a cup of herb tea would be offered. I had arrived at Irmgard's grandmother's apartment before my friend. Oma, as I called her, was delighted to see me alive. She put on a kettle of water for peppermint tea. We sat in her kitchen and chatted, and I observed that there were two heavily made up women sitting in the living room. I asked Oma if she still was the inspector for the Red Light district. She was surprised that I knew of her occupation. Then I knew that Irmgard had not told her about our sleuthing to satisfy our curiosity about her daily travels. Bravely, I added, "As a law apprentice, one learns many things." Just then, Irmgard arrived, and all three of us sat in the kitchen enjoying a cup of tea. Oma had made a second pot for the women in the living room. *"Das sind die Nutten!"* Irmgard whispered. I told her that I had spoken to her grandmother about the prostitutes. When her Oma came back into the kitchen, we told her about our plans to attend the dance lessons in the St. Pauli studio, and asked if we could meet at her apartment each time. When we noticed her reluctance, I realized that it would interfere with her routine of getting the prostitutes to the hospital for their regular checkups for VD. Irmgard immediately said, "Oma, I think it will be easier for us to go directly to the studio after all."

On one of the many commutes, I remember a particular incident. I had boarded the nearly empty trolley. Near me sat a German ex-soldier in a disheveled and torn army uniform, obviously homeless. Across from me sat a British occupation officer smoking a cigarette., which I found offensive. He was very obviously trying to attract my attention, and flirted with me outrageously. I just ignored him by avoiding eye contact. I glanced in the direction of the unfortunate derelict, to see him salivating and mesmerized by the cigarette. The officer was obviously enjoying taunting the man, and I began to find this scenario quite disgusting. I vowed that I would never permit myself to fall into such an addiction. I could not bear the sight any longer, and decided to stand at the end platform of the trolley. The Brit followed, and then puffed smoke rings in my face. I held onto a handle bar, and turned to avoid the smoke. The gaunt, emaciated soldier had followed the officer onto the platform like a rat following the Pied Piper. As the trolley came to a stop and the door opened, the Brit called out, "Here!", and flung the partly smoked reefer out of the streetcar onto the pavement. I watched in horror as the poor man dove off the trolley, and snatched up the butt just before a bystander tried to grab it.

When I got home that evening, we would have much to share at the supper table. As I came in the door, I could smell the delightful aroma of something being sauteed. Mama stood at the hearth browning onions and square slices of pressed meat. I could not believe the scent and sight of that prospective feast. "What is it?" I asked. "It's called Spam.," Mama said. Erika sat on a chair near the kitchen stove watching my mother brown the slices, then she added some cooked potatoes. What a feast we had that night! Erika proudly showed me the can the Spam had come in. It read: Pork Shoulder, Ham, Spices, and Preservatives. The manufacturer was Hormel. She reported how angry she had been to observe one particular man crawl out through the hole under the Free Harbor fence in our backyard, and proceed to traipse through her neat rows of precious vegetable seedlings, crushing them underfoot. She had previously seen the footprints through our garden, and had kept careful vigil in the hopes of catching the culprit red handed, or rather red footed. When she accosted him, he offered her part of his booty in exchange for the privilege of continuing to use the hidden egress. This serendipitous event proved to be a boon to us by providing us with additional rations for several weeks.

After dinner, I shared the latest office news with my family. My parents patted me on the back for my success, but questioned the wisdom of my tactics at the American Consulate. I also told them how the barter system at the office worked. After several civic or military trials or hearings, the individuals involved brought small parcels to give to Herr Aschermann. These packages turned out to be cartons of American cigarettes, whole bean coffee, canned goods, or baskets of fruits and vegetables. Money alone was of limited value to the society, and staples were the most highly prized commodity. I also reported that the office staff had acquired a new member in the form of a bookkeeper. He was a middle aged ex-soldier of medium height, balding, with a morose, disagreeable expression on his face. When I had been introduced to him, my eyes had fallen to his empty suit sleeve, which I later learned was the result of having lost an arm in the war. "I will be giving the orders in this office from now on, and you will be told what to do by me, Helen," he had said stiffly. Frl. Jensen was busy typing, while I was given my task for that morning, which I completed without comment. The afternoon errands were given to me in a military fashion, but I had had a chance to speak with her during one of the new bookkeeper's frequent visits to the rest room. She quickly reported that Herr Aschermann would be limiting his hours in the office in order to conserve his energy for his court appearances. I also suspected that the health of my employer limited his range of activities. Senior citizens were not the only ones to be debilitated by the rigors of the postwar conditions, as all who had survived strongly felt the enervating effects of the severely restricted diet.

Our new bookkeeper had been a German officer, and I was at first inclined to excuse his rude and peremptory behavior. I felt sorry for his affliction, but when I saw that he had a mean and sadistic streak in him, I lashed back at him. "You are not the only one who has suffered in this war," I shouted angrily, "so we should all be courteous to each other! I am not Helen to you, but Frl. Blescus!" He looked at me in astonishment, and never spoke to me again. From that point on, Frl. Jensen received a written list from him for my outside office errands, which continued for the remainder of the week. Several days later, the bookkeeper failed to appear at the office, and was never heard from again.

Irmgard and I met at the dance studio, which was located on the Seilerstrasse, in the St. Pauli district, in a large, wood-floored hall. A chesty, full figured woman wearing a long, dark gown greeted us from the center of the room. On either side, several dozen chairs stood lined up against the walls. *Die Frau Tanzdirektorin*, or *Frigatte*, as Irmgard called her, motioned for us to take seats on the ladies' side. The boys and young men already sat eyeing the new arrivals. The son of the director came gliding into the room like a blond Rudolph Valentino, dressed in a tuxedo. He had sleek golden hair, and had bedroom eyes, as Irmgard said. "He's a real gigolo type, if I ever saw one," she remarked. The mother was poised like a ship's figurehead, with her large bosom protruding, waiting for her son to guide her across the dance floor. After they had demonstrated the steps of a fox trot to the accompaniment of a Victrola, the gentlemen were instructed to approach the ladies, bow, and request a dance. This resulted in a minor stampede, and two males vied for my hand as partner. I hesitated, not wanting to offend either of them, and waited for instructions in protocol from our dance mistress. She saw my predicament, and chose a shy, red-haired boy who had lagged behind the others. The poor lad, who was an auto mechanic, had arrived directly from work with grease still under his fingernails.

He sweated profusely, and his pale skin turned deep red as he approached me. In his awkward attempts at dancing, he pushed me across the floor as if he were driving a Jeep. I hoped that our dance instructors would let us change partners for the next lesson, but that did not happen for several sessions. Each session started with the mother and son couple demonstrating the various steps we were to learn. The son would then pick one of the students to provide a further example. He always chose the same overly made up partner, whom Irmgard described as *die zukünftige Nutte* (the prospective hooker). Irmgard and I quickly learned the foxtrot, waltz, two-step, and the rudiments of the Argentinian tango. My red-headed partner barely managed to acquire the *Schieber* (two-step), and was totally unable to master any of the other dances. As soon as each lesson was over, I had to dash off like Cinderella, to catch the ferry in order to be home before curfew.

ON ONE FRIDAY, as I reached the cottage, I saw my mother and sister waiting for me in the front garden. "He took Papa!" They called out hysterically. Both were crying and talking at once . My mother was in shock as she described what had transpired. As I put my arm around her and felt the sobs racking her body, I realized how much the years of exposure to living under the stressful, sleepless, sanity-robbing conditions had taken toll on her. We sat down on the brick steps which Papa had just converted from wood the week before. Erika then added details to the story. It seems that the ex-Gestapo man had pushed his way into the house, and insisted on waiting for Papa while he proceeded to search through the kitchen for contraband. He saw the now nearly empty can of Spam, and when Papa arrived, he immediately arrested him for stealing an Allied occupation force product. I asked Erika if she knew where they had taken him, but my mother, who by now was sufficiently calm, answered, "That devil and his dog took Papa away, I do not know to where." We stayed up all night discussing what to do. We decided to ask Herr Aschermann for help, but he did not expect me in the office until Monday morning, and there was no telephone available anywhere in the area. Over the weekend, I walked to the soccer field, hoping to see Helmut, who was frequently to be found there on his free time. I knew some of his comrades, and told them to let him know that I wished to speak with him. The efficient medium of word of mouth worked well again. Helmut knocked on our door that afternoon, and reported that my father, as well as several other men, had been arrested and taken by military truck to the city center, but he did not know exactly where.

The following Monday, I immediately described what had happened to my father to my employer. Herr Aschermann personally made several phone calls, but could not discover my father's whereabouts. He assured me that he would do everything in his power to find Papa. When I came home from work, Mama reported that she had visited the Neuhof police station, which was located in the center of our two neighborhood housing blocks. She had stormed into the office of that "*Schweinehund*", and the years of emotions pent up in a totalitarian environment broke all dams, and the veneer of courtesy that Mama had always maintained, broke. "Helen, if I would have had a weapon, I would have killed that bastard!" To this day, I firmly believed that she would have been capable of doing just that, given her agitated frame of mind. My poor mother, who had left her Hamburg birthplace, like so many North Europeans who had emmigrated to America from this largest port of debarkation, had been driven to search for a better way of life. After struggling to establish a home and family in America, she had to decide to give up all to accompany my father back to Germany because of his illegal status and subsequent deportation. Even as a young child in our Bethpage, Long Island home, I could not understand why my hard working father had to leave the USA simply because he had jumped ship in this country to find his own errant father. All for the lack of a visa, a piece of bureaucratically devised paper! Our detention in Germany had been a forced situation in any case, and to have this latest outrage perpetrated upon us was almost totally unbearable. I commiserated with my mothers frustration, and assured her that Herr Aschermann would be able to help us find out where Papa was being detained, and obtain his release.

In the meantime, I walked with Erika towards Wilhelmsburg each morning, where I boarded the water taxi to commute to work, and she proceeded to her school. Mama tended her vegetable and herb garden in front of our cottage, while all the Neuhof residents passed to and fro. There were the shipyard workers, crews of the various merchant ships docked inside the Free Harbor, and girls who worked at the fish factory. As Mama weeded and hoed her neat rows of seedlings, neighbors and seamen stopped to chat with her. In the evenings, as we sat around our pot of *Eintopf* (soup), the latest news was exchanged. My mother told us of the sailors who had passed by, and were headed for the only tavern on Neuhof, near the police station. These men of the sea were usually the ones who were family oriented, looking for local contact to "shoot the breeze", as my father liked to put it, rather than the other element who preferred to catch the water taxis to the *Landungsbrücken* to visit the *Reeperbahn* entertainment center. This area was to be the site of the first gigs of the Beetles group many years later. It included the Hamburg "Broadway" of shooting galleries, the famous *Zillertal* beer hall, sleazy, as well as respectable cafés, theaters, kinos, and the red light district, which was located on side streets off the main drag. *Die Grosse Freiheit* district had opened some nightclubs with telephones on each table, and Elfriede's mother was our chaperone on one afternoon excursion, after we had met, as previously arranged, in Café Giese. We sat down at numbered tables with our soft drinks. When the telephone rang, Elfriede's mother would answer it, and ask which table the caller was sitting at. She would then look over to check out the male, and if she felt that his telephone manner as well as his appearance were satisfactory to her and to either of us, the caller would then be permitted to speak with the brunette Elfriede or the blond Helen. We found it to be great amusement at first, but when the chatter turned to meeting outside of the club, I discouraged it.

However, this only made one young fellow quite ardent in pursuit. After saying my *Auf Wiedersehen* to my friends to leave the club in order to catch the ferry home before curfew, I felt that I was being followed. The trolley to the *Landungsbrücken* stood at the corner, so I hopped aboard, only to see that the young telephone caller was just as quick. When I got off at the ferry pier, he walked towards me. "Please, may I see you again?" He pleaded. "I'm sorry, but that's quite impossible," I said firmly. "Why not?" he countered. I hesitated, and tried to think of a good excuse, but also not to hurt his feelings. "I have very little time to socialize; study and work are my life." "How fortunate you are to have such passions!" he answered. "Where does it come from? Certainly not out of these piles of rubble. Can I at least walk part way to your destination?" That, I permitted, for I knew that I had to catch my ferry to get back home before the siren announced curfew. He had to live somewhere in the harbor district of the city, I reasoned, and would not follow me onto the ferry. If he did, I could always solicit the aid of the captain or one of the crew if the stranger became a pest.

"All right, so be it for now!" I remember answering Peter, who had introduced himself with that name on the nightclub telephone. While we sat on the bench at the *Landungsbrücken* waiting for my vessel, Peter told me his life story. As another young German, he had been drafted into the *Kriegsmarine*, and served in the Atlantic theater aboard a U-boat. After being captured by the British,, he was pressed into service on a mine sweeper, to clear the North Sea, the English Channel, and parts of the North Atlantic. He now lived in a sailor's home near the *Grüne Michel*. "You are making it possible for me to soon cross the Atlantic to return home to my America," were the last words I spoke to Peter before I boarded the *Harburger* ferry. On board the vessel, I chatted with the crew as I stood by the rail watching their hawser procedures upon departure. Peter stood at the pier, waving his handkerchief, pretending to cry, or was it for real?

Another Dance of Life

"Next Sunday, the submarine bunker is going to be dynamited!" I heard the deck hand call out to me. "The *Harburger Dampfer* will not be keeping its schedule. I thought you would like to know."

I was the only one to get off at Neuhof. It was a beautiful evening, and I again strolled towards my beach. I walked along the sand, and wondered when I would see Coney Island again. Then I turned to hurry home before curfew. Mama and Erika had been working in the garden, but were resting on the brick steps when I arrived. Erika had Moochie, my birthday cat from Elfriede, on her lap. The cat got up, stretched, and greeted me like a dog would. Of course, instead of wagging her tail, she meowed and schmoozed against my legs. I bent down to stroke and praise her, then sat down next to my mother and sister, and took her onto my lap. I told them about my visit with Elfriede and her mother, and the poor ex*Kriegsmarine* sailor who had the dangerous job of blowing up mines, and that the ferry deck hand had told me of the plans to dynamite the submarine bunker next week. We went into the cottage as the alarm siren announced curfew. Each of us took turns sponging ourselves with water heated on the stove. The used water was put into the swab pail for Mama's plants. Then we climbed the ladder, one by one, Erika first, then I, then my mother. I could not sleep, but thought of the events of the day. The sad eyes of Peter, who had lost his mother in a bombing raid, and did not know if his father had been killed on the Russian front, or was being held prisoner in Siberia. Then I heard my mother crying in the other bedroom, and the tears came to my eyes as well.

The next morning, I was the first to climb down the ladder and open the outside door to let in the cat. I left the door open after calling Moochie several times, as she did not appear to be around yet. I then stirred the hearth fire to heat the morning kettle of water for our face wash and ersatz coffee. Mama then joined me in the kitchen. We both heard a loud thump against the window, heard the cat meowing, and then spotted her sitting on the outside sill. Mama went to the door, and beckoned as well as called the cat to

119

come in. She just meowed louder, and began prancing back and forth on the ground in front of the window. Finally, we both went outside to see what the cat was up to, as she usually was quick to respond to our calls by running into the house to huddle near the kitchen stove. There, beneath the window, were three dead mice lined up in a careful row, obviously laid out for us to inspect. We petted and praised her. When we failed to pick up her offering, she proceeded to carry them into the kitchen, again laying them neatly in a row in front of the hearth. I know this sounds like the typical cat owner's boast of implying human qualities to an animal, but the deed was really so obvious as to be incapable of misinterpretation. "My God," my mother said, "she really wants us to eat them! We have never had enough food, other than water and grits to give her, and now she wants to provide us! I remember when, as a child in WWI, a butcher was arrested for having added rat and mouse meat to his sausages. Who knows what they put into our wurst rations today?" Erika came down the ladder and played with Moochie till our morning grits was served. My mother picked up the dead mice while Erika was distracting the cat, and threw them onto the compost heap. The grits had been standing in the *Kochkiste* overnight, and was now fully cooked. The grain was still part of the sack Papa and I had recovered from the Elbe.

Mama planned to visit the Neuhof police station to plead with one of the bureaucrats whom Helmut had recommended contacting regarding Papa's whereabouts. I braided Erika's hair, and we then walked towards Wilhelmsburg together while my mother walked in the opposite direction. I hopped on board the water taxi, and Erika continued walking to her school. When I arrived at work, Herr Aschermann had still not received word from any of his various sources about my father. I went on with my daily routine, much like a windup mechanical doll. I shuttled per trolley through the grey rubble of the city to deliver or pick up the various reams of paperwork from the interior of the government buildings, which the morose office clerks had either stamped, denied, accepted, or returned for me to file on my employer's shelves in alphabetical order. That evening when I returned from work, I found Helmut standing at the ferry stop. He knew my weekday schedule, even though we seldom saw each other. I was alarmed to see him, for each of us had our separate life styles, and I suspected by his facial expression that he might be going to report some unpleasant news. "What is it?" I asked immediately. "That bastard came to your cottage with a truck, and forced himself into your home. They have confiscated all your father's tools. Your mother and Erika are in despair. I promised them I would meet you at the ferry." We solemnly hurried along the Nippoldstrasse together. The nosy neighbors gave us that all-knowing look. When we arrived at the center of the block where I thought Helmut and his family lived, I thanked him for his concern. It was important to me to keep every man interested in me at arm length's distance. We had a fine romance holding hands once in a while, with an occasional goodnight kiss, for I heeded my mother's quote that *"Küssen ist keine Sünd'"* (kissing is no sin), from the song made famous by the Viennese tenor Richard Tauber. Mama was working in the garden, and Erika was sitting on the stoop with the cat on her lap when I arrived. My mother stopped her work when she saw me, and beckoned me into the cottage, leaving my sister to play with the cat. Her eyes were red rimmed from crying, but she was now under control of her emotions. She opened the door to the room that was to be the parlor, but for now was still Papa's work shop and our storage for food, water, wood, and coal. The room was empty, except for the containers filled with water. I gasped at seeing everything that we had so carefully bartered and worked for gone, including the presents of cartons of cigarettes from Papa's merchant seamen acquaintances, and the contraband canned goods the harbor workers had given us in exchange for the privilege of crossing through our property. My mother then related how the ex-Gestapo man had forced his way in, and, together with the truck driver, had proceeded to remove the entire contents of the room without any explanation. I now became very angry, and we decided to go to the police station to demand accountability for this outrageous violation of our civil rights.

"The tools with the company's name on them is all the evidence I need. The empty cans of Spam and other products have been returned to the Allied Forces," he laughed sadistically. "Go home before curfew keeps you here in our custody. Tomorrow, the Military Police will come, and who knows what they will do to you?" Mama and I just looked at each other, and turned to leave. "Have a good evening, ladies," he called out. We later found out that he himself had simply kept all of our possessions.

After a most restless night, we got Erika ready for school. I had decided to stay home to support Mama, when the MP jeep drove up. My mother saw them as Erika reluctantly walked towards Wilhelmsburg without me that morning. The two Redcaps greeted us courteously, and Mama asked them if they would like a cup of herb tea. They accepted gratefully, and we sat around the kitchen table, which was covered with the blue checked cloth, while we sat silently in embarrassment. After they had sipped the tea, the senior officer took a pad from his pocket, and asked us our names, ages, address, and places of birth. When I told him mine was in New York City, they almost in unison said, "So, you are the Yankee girl we've heard about!" Now I had the courage to give them a complete picture of what had happened since the Allied Forces had marched in: "During the no-man's land period, my father and I, along with many others, had gone to the Submarine Base, which had been abandoned. My father went to his work station, and I to the supply depot, where I was among the last to enter, and managed to find a few leftover items that had not been picked over and the rest spoiled by those ahead of me. Even then, I got chased by two British soldiers who confiscated most of what I had scrounged. My father, in the meantime, had taken some hand tools with which to build this house on this piece of property, which was just a gigantic bomb crater. He single handedly disposed of the bomb dud which still lay buried in the bottom of the pit. Noone else had the gumption to tackle that kind of a project! My sister and I spent many months cleaning up bricks from the rubble of the housing block. Mama worked hard to cultivate the land to supplement the meager rations allotted us by the Allies. We desperately need the upcoming harvest to survive, now that that Gestapo scoundrel has deprived us of all our stored foods and gifts from others." The two men scratched their heads, took a deep breath, and looked even more embarrassed than before. As they got up, the officer said, "We have to inspect the rear of the property to check on the damage to the Free Harbor fence."

That afternoon, after the Redcaps had left, my mother and I took turns stationing ourselves near the gap in the backyard fence, pretending to be busy with gardening. We knew that this would be our last chance to extract tolls from the workers smuggling out staples from the base and supply ships. On my watch, a coworker of my father's dropped a can of Holland cheese, tipped his hat, and I thankfully picked up what was to be my last booty.

The next morning, after I had left for work, an Allied repair crew drove up and labored all day to straighten out the fence and fill in the hole. Several days later, the British senior officer dropped by to tell my mother that he had located Papa, and had had him transferred to a hospital. We still did not know where or why, but were much relieved to have the information. Now at least knowing my father's situation, I needed to approach the Hamburg Free Hanseatic legal department to determine his exact whereabouts. The person who could help me, would be Irmgard's father. He had worn many hats in the city. I knew that he had been the owner of an apartment house and the business of a *Gastwirtschaft*, plus now being an official in the *Rathaus*, where I had recently met him. The following Friday, I related all to Irmgard when I met her for our last dance session. She promised to tell her father, but also invited me to come to Waltershof for a visit. Hopefully, by that time, she would have the information I was seeking.

That day, as luck, or rather bad luck, would have it, was the day that the submarine bunker was to be demolished. It was a most memorable event, with lots of extra British military police, as well as Allied demolition experts, flooding our area. I had borrowed my father's bicycle, which stood covered with a tarpaulin in the back of the house. Miraculously, the Gestapo agent had overlooked it. I hated to ride a man's bike, as the cross bar made wearing a dress awkward. I only liked to wear the bell-bottomed trousers in the winter for warmth, and had no summer pedal pushers or slacks for warm weather. Dressed in skirt and sweater, I rode off to catch the flat bottomed work vessel to Waltershof. The army of soldiers whistled, cheered, and hooted as I cycled past them onto the ferry. There was never any regular time schedule for the ferry, and it simply crossed and re-crossed the channel all day. I reached Waltershof in just a few minutes. Narrow paths crossed a large area which was systematically divided into small parcels of land. Low wire fences bordered with berry bushes, rows of flowers or fruit trees, were the barriers delineating each property owner's garden. The Scheel's piece of land was in the center of these divisions. When I arrived, I opened the gate and pushed my bike through. I heard loud barking. Irmgard stood at the open window at the front of the house, still washing the noon meal dishes. "Stay where you are; don't come any closer!" she shouted. Then I saw her come out of the front door, reeling in the chains of two Doberman Pinchers. She gave them sharp orders, and then locked them in a small kennel next to the *Behelfsheim*, as the structure was called, since she, like us, had lost their previous home in the July 1943 bombing. "My parents are napping, but I told my father everything you related to me. He will try to find your father's whereabouts, now that we at least know that he's in a hospital." Then we chatted about our dance sessions at Madame *Frigatte's* and her gigolo son's studio, the awkward dance partners we each had, and the upcoming maskerade ball to be held at the *Alsterhaus*. Marion had invited me, perhaps she could also get a ticket for Irmgard. However, the Allied soldiers hoped to share the event with us, and I asked her if she had studied her English any further. Of course, she had not, and her father was definitely not in favor of having her attend the party. "That reminds me," I said, "Günther Morgenroth, our previous neighbor, keeps asking me about you. He's the very healthy looking fellow whose mother shielded him during the war, telling all that he had TB." Irmgard shook her head and said, "I do not want to be involved with a sick boy!" I answered, "Remember how your father kept you out of the Hitler Youth? Didn't he say you were a sickly child, and regrettably could not come to *Dienst*?" We then said our Auf Wiedersehen, and I pedaled through the maze of *Schrebergärten*. When I reached the main road towards the ferry, I saw a Jeep standing by the roadside, with three soldiers in it. As I passed by, they whistled and called out, "Stop, Blondie, and come for a ride with us!" I saw bottles in the back seat, and could tell by their erratic demeanor that they were already drunk, and up to no good. I pedaled hard, hoping to reach the street to the ferry, where the crew or other passengers might see me. The Jeep cut me off before I could reach that road, so I swerved sharply to the side, and spun out on the coarse gravel. The men's bike bar prevented me from jumping off quickly, and my bare leg hit the gravel, with my knee digging into the ground and being severely scraped. I screamed in rage and pain. The soldiers had stopped the Jeep a few yards away from me, and sat stupefied. "Stay where you are!" I now shouted, and, lifting myself from under the bike, I laboriously hobbled to the ferry. An old fashioned, long handled water pump stood near the station, and I awkwardly proceeded to soak my handkerchief and clean my wound. Slowly, and with great difficulty, I pushed my bike aboard the ferry. In a few minutes, we had crossed over to Neuhof, and I saw that the U-boat bunker had been demolished. The throngs of soldiers and demolition experts were all gone, and the area was completely covered in dust from the explosions. The walk back to the housing block was painful, but pushing the bike offered me some support. Only a few people were hanging out in front of the various doors of the apartment houses. Günther spotted me as I schlepped by, and asked what had happened to me. "I fell," I remember answering simply, and continued on my way without stopping for further conversation. Just before reaching our cottage, some merchant seamen came towards me. Helga and some of her coworkers from the fish factory were strolling along with them. Helga and I often chatted briefly, while we walked or happened to meet aboard one of the harbor vessels on our ways to a kino. Movies played a major role in cheering us up, and the newsreels helped to inform us of current events. The Neuhof fish factory girls were notorious for falling in love with a different man each week. Often, before I could even see them, the strong odor of fish would precede them. Then I could hear them talking, accompanied by their fish scent. They were hopeless romantics. I listened to their latest infatuations, and their anticipation and belief in *die Grosse Liebe*, but the following days or weeks later, all their romantic dreams of the Great Love had evaporated. Some thought that the next fellow would surely be The One, but for most, it was usually a bittersweet ending. Helga never seemed to learn. One day, she would be happy and madly in love, the next day she would be in tears, weeping uncontrollably, vowing never to trust a man again. However, that conviction never seemed to last long. Their experiences were great lessons for me. My determination was to reach my goal of having a foundation for a career in place for my homecoming to America. I knew that I would have to earn a living for myself when I got back to New York. As I limped by Helga, one of the men called out, "Are you Helena? Me, Nick the Greek. I know your Papa." I stopped, curious at how he knew my father. "Me meet him many weeks ago, he built that house!" The seaman was pointing at our cottage. He then came closer to assist me, offered to push the bike with his left arm, and supported me with his right arm. My home was within sight, and I spotted my mother and sister in the front garden. Mama thanked the man for helping me, and he returned to the group standing by the roadside. They then continued on their way to the local tavern. Mama became alarmed upon seeing the deep gashes in my knee and the bruises on my arm from the accident. She heated water on the stove, put some in a dishpan, and carefully made a thick, sudsy lather with the Lux soap I had exchanged for my Navaho ring. We did not have any alcohol or other disinfectant, not even cotton pads, bandaids, tape or safety pins, only a wash cloth and two large white handkerchiefs. As a bandage, Mama tore off a strip from the blue and white checked table cloth, and wrapped it around my knee. I was propped up on the day bed in front of our table, and told to keep my leg up. My mother immediately assumed her role as nurse, and made me a strong cup of peppermint tea. She proceeded to blame my mishap on my adventurous spirit, from riding my father's bicycle, to crossing the *Süder Elbe* on a day when we knew that the bunker was to be dynamited. "You couldn't stay home with us! Why in the world did you have to go to Waltershof? Now look at your knee! Let's hope it doesn't get infected."

The next morning, I limped to the water taxi station, while Erika continued on to the Wilhemsburg school. In a hypnotic state, I went through my daily chores. Only in the afternoon did my employer notice the bandage around my knee. I told him what had happened, and hoped that my friend's father could find out which hospital my father would be in. Again, Herr Aschermann assured me he was looking into the matter. He told me to go home early, and take the next few days off to allow my knee, as well as my left arm, which had become stiff from the fall, to heal. My mother was glad to see me arrive home earlier than usual. Erika reported, that just as she had walked by the Free Harbor gate, she had encountered Nick-the-Greek, who gave her a box of food to bring home to us. "Watch out no let the cato have it!" he said to her, and asked if he could come by that evening, after his duty on board. We appreciated the delicious meal that perhaps he had himself prepared, and wondered if he were the ship's cook. Since my parents had a Nick-the-Greek friend in New York, my mother was already familiar with Greek dishes. The Greek friend in America was married to Florence, a German descent woman who had taken care of me soon after I had been weaned, and when my parents had been working on an estate in Litchfield, Connecticut. Nick had a restaurant in Queens, New York, and I believe that I had often been taken there, for when I, many years later, became interested in Mid-Eastern dance, the strains of Greek music seemed somehow quite familiar to me. Well, that evening, the second Nick-the-Greek showed up at our house. My mother welcomed him into our cottage. Again, he gave us a bag of food, but also had brought along a deck of cards and a bottle of strong Greek liquor. We politely asked him how he knew my father, and we learned that it had been through an over-the-fence conversation at our building site. Papa had spoken with many passers by from the various ship's crews and shipyard workers during the time when he was building our cottage. After we had eaten, Nick asked us if we knew how to play cards. My parents knew various games, such as pinochle and gin rummy, and my sister and I had learned from them, so we decided on gin rummy. Erika, in fact, had become quite proficient in shuffling, fanning, and flicking cards, and I watched in fascination as she dealt. I mostly daydreamed during the games, thinking of what to do when I returned to the USA with her. I would become an owner of a Mississippi river boat, and she would be the card shark. We would collect at least 20% of the daily takes, and would be able to purchase Scarlett O'Hara's southern mansion, and live happily ever after. We would have great musical events featuring international musicians and ethnic dancers of many countries. Then we would have an Italian grape-stomping festival, with wine tasting and all the food you could eat. I would arrange a Viennese ball with my own Strauss orchestra for another event, or a *Schützenfest*, perhaps even a reenactment of a mediaeval tournament, or a rodeo with country and western music. All these events would, of course, be accompanied by the most delectable dishes imaginable. "Come on, Helen, let's get on with the game," my mother reminded me, arousing me from my fantasies. Begrudgingly, I played my hand. Nick was sitting next to me, filling his glass again and again from the bottle he had brought along. For the third or fourth time, my mother and I declined to drink with him. I really disliked playing cards, and went back to my daydreaming. Now, I revived the Hamburg sailing ship

Reederei F. Laeisz. The descendants must still be around, I mused. After the Allied soldiers and American citizens had sailed home on the troop ships, sailing vessels might be employed to let the people who want to emigrate be brought to the American continent, as in earlier days. My grandma Abt-Schröder on my mother's side had relatives in Buffalo, New York. On my grandfather's side were the Friedrichs and Sängers, scattered across the USA, only Tante Guste really knew where, but for some reason always jealously guarded that information. Our only solid contact was Uncle Hans, my father's older brother, but in view of the destruction of all of our former residences, as well as his probable relocation, we wondered how we would be able to find each other. Also, in spite of the vast and usually efficient German bureaucracy, would a communication be forwarded to our present address? We did not even know the whereabouts of my father at this time. How could we ever expect to establish contact with Uncle Hans? "Helen, it's your turn, pay attention to the game!" Erika admonished me. I played my hand, and returned to my musings. Since I had taken every opportunity to inspect every ocean liner my father had worked on before the bombings, I wondered if the remaining steam vessels could not be refurbished? I had seen the stacks of the blue ribbon winner *Bremen* peeking out from the skyline of Waltershof, and wondered if I could myself stimulate interest in having the vessel recommissioned. Then again, what would happen to the sail training ships Gorch Fock and Horst Wessel that I had visited while they lay in the harbor at Kiel in 1942. Much later, after my return to the U.S., and when I was living in Mystic, CT, I chanced to meet Captain Gordon McGowan, author of the book *The Skipper and the Eagle*. The U.S. Coast Guard had been far sighted enough to acquire the Horst Wessel as a war prize, renaming it *Eagle*, and commissioned Captain McGowan to deliver it to the Academy at New London, CT, to be used for the training of Coast Guard officers and crew.

Now, I felt a touch on my leg, which aroused me from my daydreaming. At first, I thought it an accident, but when I looked down, I saw Nick's hand on my knee. I gave him a sharp kick, and at the same time announced that I no longer wished to play. "Yes," Mama said, "Nick, it's time for you to return to your ship. It's almost curfew time. Please leave!" He just sat there in a drunken stupor, staring at the now empty bottle, then toppled over, his face hitting the table. The three of us just looked at each other in surprise. "What are we going to do?" Mama asked. Erika opted for simply pushing him out of the door. However, his herbivorous build was too much for us to handle. "Just let him sit there. We can be safe after we have climbed up to the bedrooms. All we have to do, is pull up the ladder," I suggested to Mama. She thought that was a good solution. We climbed to the second floor, and quietly pulled up the ladder. We laughed, and thought this a marvelously comic solution. "Like a castle under siege, there's no way he can get to us from down below." We had convinced ourselves of that, but Mama said that she would never-the-less keep watch. Erika giggled, and we all went to bed. I soon fell asleep, since my injuries made me tired and listless. I slept late the following morning, and did not hear Erika get up. I did not have to go to work, and was thankful that I could rest. Mama and Erika had lowered the ladder after they heard Nick stumble out of the door.

That afternoon, we had a surprise visitor. My Aunt Else, my father's youngest sister, had arrived from Kiel, and had brought along a letter from Uncle Hans. This was most exciting news, indeed! We forgot all about our previous night's experience. Tante Else and her husband Albert Köpke were fortunate in not having lost their home in the bombings, therefor, they had not suffered the displacements we had endured. I still remember her excitement as we read the letter over and over again. We now knew Uncle Hans' address, and that would be the last requirement, I thought, the American Consulate would need. I still remembered my Aunt Grete's words when I had pleaded with my uncle to let me remain with them, rather than to go to Germany with my parents and sister. She had insisted that they bring over her son from a previous marriage in Germany before she would be willing to have me stay with them. Now, however, they wanted to know how they could help us. We were all in great spirits at this news, except, still not knowing of my father's whereabouts, we could not provide him with this encouraging communication.

Else also brought us up to date on the latest happenings with the rest of the family. Her sister Betty, a professional bookbinder, and her marine engineer husband Herbert had been having marital difficulties. How sad, I thought, what wonderful times I had with them at the large apartment on the Ringstrasse in Kiel. One time, when I was on a visit, Uncle Herbert had been recuperating from a serious operation. Nothing cheered him up as much as when we played the popular German board game *Mensch, Ärgere Dich Nicht*. I, of course, aggravated myself on losing so often, while he would laugh so hard he had to bend over to avoid having his stitches burst. Tante Betty worked for a publishing house which had been converted to print ration cards. One Christmas, she had made me a hand bound leather address book with my initials stamped in gold. I treasured this until, unfortunately, it was lost in the bombing. After a few days of being house bound, Uncle Herbert had wanted to get back into shape by first *Spazierengehen*, and then we soon all joined him in his brisk walks. Both of my aunts and I enjoyed *Wandern*, or hiking, and we all laughed and often sang the wandering Miller song, *Das Wandern ist des Müller's Lust*. The two sisters and their husbands all had secure and interesting occupations with many fringe benefits, such as long vacations, and health insurance, which included weeks of Resort Spa privileges. On weekends, before the hardships of war robbed us of our peaceful existence, they and I would often bicycle through Kiel to the Baltic Sea. We stopped along the way in quaint villages with thatched roof farm houses, throughout Schleswig-Holstein, or viewed the Kaiser Wilhelm Canal. Uncle Herbert had built a beautiful two seat lapstrake kayak. Tante Betty and I paddled in it, while he raced ahead of us in his single seat *Faltboot*. Most of the year, they kept their craft in a boat house which was part of an attractive club restaurant in a park-like setting overlooking the Kieler harbor. However, for the two summer months of July and August, the club rented an island in the Plöner Lake. I spent wonderful vacations camping, swimming, and kayaking with them and other members of the club. My father frequently referred to them all as the *Sportler*, for they were exclusively dedicated to sports. They were also excellent gymnasts, highly interested in the Olympics, and had many interesting stories to tell about the 1936 event. My father also showed off his athletic ability by walking on his hands, or performing complex dives from the high board at the local *Badeanstalt*. Tante Betty and Uncle Herbert, once or twice a year, would stop by our apartment house with skis on their shoulders, on the way to entrain for alpine slopes. Tante Else was an enthusiastic mountain climber and swimmer, and was a life-long member of the Kieler *Turnverein*. At an age of 36, she was becoming concerned that her biological clock would be ticking down because of the cumulative stresses of the war. Uncle Albert still worked for the city of Kiel, which provided them with an attractive townhouse style apartment in the Kiel suburb of Elmschenhagen. The building stood on one of the corners where the weekly outdoor market took place. To me, it was always like a Grimm's fairy tale location; a two story red brick building with a small terrace in the rear, and a long garden. The homes, though attached, offered complete privacy. My only cousin, Margret, was born there after I had returned to the U.S.. I thought her fortunate to be raised in that environment.

Now I would be the first of my family to return to America. My aunt lamented that it was a shame that my grandfather had never been found there. "Yes," I replied, "however that is why Papa and Uncle Hans became seamen. The objective had been to find their father, however, Papa would not have met Mama, and I would not have been born." We all laughed. "Well, the war is now over, and hopefully, a solution to rebuild this devastated land will be found."

Tante Else stayed the night, and slept in my parent's bedroom. Erika and I heard them talking until way past midnight. "Will you send both of the girls to New York?" I held my breath while waiting for my mother to answer. After a long pause, she said, "No, Helen will go alone. However, I would prefer her to stay, since she is assured of a law position and a study program at the Hamburg University. But, it is more important for her to receive proper nutrition and decent clothing at this time in her life. She also is very homesick for America." Erika just sighed, and went to sleep. I lay awake for hours, but when I finally fell asleep, I had pleasant dreams of my ship sailing into the New York harbor, with music playing, flags waving, and the fire boats spraying streams of water in the air. Along the pier, a large banner with Welcome Home was strung across the building.

"*Aufstehen!*" my mother's voice rang out. "We're taking Tante Else to the Altonaer *Hauptbahnhof* to catch the train to Kiel. After that, we'll go to Irmgard Timm, my dress maker friend, to have some clothes made for you from material I exchanged for jewelry and cigarettes." "Lucky you," Erika commented. We both dressed quietly. Then, before we left the loft, she asked, "Did you hear anything more of what the two were talking about?" I did not tell her that Tante Else had been in touch with Hans-Egon, the son of Tante Grete. It seems that he had been drafted into the Wehrmacht, and, during the last year of the war, had married, and was now living in Solingen.

We had a pleasant trip into Hamburg aboard the Harburger Paddle wheel ferry. It eased up to the Landungsbrücken, where we were again confronted with the appalling desolation of the city. Tante Else commented, "I still can imagine how beautiful Hamburg used to be. I just wonder how long it will take to be rebuilt, and when the work will get under way." "I will not be around to see it being built up again. Tomorrow, I'm going to the American Consul with Uncle Hans' address. I'm leaving as soon as I can!"

We said goodby to Tante Else at the Altonaer train station, and I did not see her again for ten years, when I met my only cousin Margret for the first time, when she was seven years old.

Irma Timm, one of my mother's Pinneberg relatives, answered the buzzer at the apartment building off the Bahrenfelder Strasse when my mother pressed the button. She was delighted to see us. Mama told her that she had two pieces of material, and asked what could be made out of it for me. Irma invited us first to have some ersatz coffee and some *Kuchen* she had saved in a tin box for such a special occasion. She again related the terrible story of her husband's release from a Russian Gulag. Only German prisoners-of-war too ill to work were released and sent back home. Herr Timm was one of the dubiously lucky ones to be put onto a train bound for Hamburg, but he was so sick, that even with the fervent exhortations of his comrades, he was unable to ward off the grim reaper. Irma had stood at the Altonaer Bahnhof with her two daughters, but only ten minutes before pulling into the station, he had died. Elke and Ingrid sat opposite Erika and me, tears streaming down their cheeks. We all began to cry, and Mama then related how the ex-Gestapo man, now head of the Neuhof police, had taken our food, tools, and other commodities from our cottage. My father had then been pounced upon as he came home from work, and we still did not know where he was. "Under what pretext did that scoundrel enter your house?" Irma asked. "He wanted to see the inside of our cottage, for he said he was interested in hiring Papa to build him a place two *Schrebergärten* from us," Mama replied. "Once he was inside our kitchen/ living room, he saw some American canned goods on the shelves, and then brazenly proceeded to open cupboards. He found the empty containers with English labels we were using to store such items as my dried herbs, tea mixtures, nails, pins, or other odds and ends. Since Neuhof did not provide any garbage collection, and we could not buy any utensils or domestic products, Erich and I used any and all cans and containers to store things. Whatever garbage we had was deposited onto my compost heap for the garden. All these things had been given to us by Erich's seamen friends, or left as tokens by the enterprising workers who had used the hole under our back fence to leave the Free Harbor. We then saw that a truck was standing in front of our house, and realized that the ex-Gestapo man had used his reason to enter our house merely as a ploy, and had intended all along to deprive us of whatever he felt he could get away with." Irma was equally appalled, and commented on how outrageous an act that was. "Is their no justice?" Now it was my turn to interject. "As a law apprentice, I have interviewed many of the men who wanted my employer to represent them. These were all poor souls who had been locked up in the basement jails of the courthouse. Only the wealthy, lucky ones could get a quick trial. Even with all my own contacts, I have been unable to find Papa's whereabouts. Tomorrow, when I go to the American Consulate with Uncle Hans' address, I will take the opportunity to make further inquiries." I still had some vestiges of confidence in my ability to sniff out some information, and desperately hoped to be able to find my father before I departed to the U.S.A.. Irma nodded in agreement. "The good news," my mother said, "is that my sister-in-law has heard from Hans, Erich's brother in America, so we are planning on sending Helen across the ocean by herself." She then carefully took out a piece of green and black plaid rayon, and a few yards of patterned white cloth. I was not particularly excited about either materials. "Well," Irma sighed, "let Helen pick out the patterns. She's artistic. I'll listen to what she has in mind." I looked over all the dress patterns she had, and finally chose one for the rayon material, but I wanted the cotton to have made into a skirt and jacket, provided there was sufficient cloth. Irma took my measurements, and we set a date for the first fitting for the following week.

In the meantime, I undertook the task of repairing the only pair of black pumps I had. My father had bartered some of his tools for a shoemaker's last, because we were forced to do our own shoe repairs. I set up the last, and although I had already been successful in replacing heels on various pairs, I now attempted to sole the pumps with some leather my father had acquired. After soaking the leather, I used an awl to puncture holes along the edges, and then proceeded to hammer in wooden pegs. I was not happy with the results, and fastened the rest of the sole using upholstery tacks. Although this method seemed to serve for the interim, I was later to be plagued by the tacks protruding through the soles into my feet. Papa had also carved me a pair of wooden soles, to which I attached straps I had crocheted from odds and ends of yarn. They were quite functional, but certainly not very stylish. Besides having to do our own shoe repairs, my mother and I were continually engaged in mending our clothes, particularly our undergarments. Elastic was not available, and we were obliged to use string instead. One amusing incident resulting from this practice occurred when a string on my panties broke as I was walking down the *Mönkebergerstrasse*. They fell to the ground, and I ducked into a nearby hallway after picking them up. As I pondered my dilemma, a man's hand appeared from around the corner holding a safety pin. I gratefully accepted this beau geste, but although I never saw my knight in shining armor, the telltale trail of ashes on the ground and the scraping sound of ashcans led me to surmise that it had been the trash collector.

Besides the need to repair our clothes, an activity my mother and I assiduously and regularly applied ourselves to, our greatest recreation was reading. We, of course had lost all of our own books, and the kind of libraries available were to be found at local grocery stores, which devoted a few shelves for book rentals. Other sources of reading materials were in the nature of exchanges and loans from friends and teachers. In order to keep these treasures in as good a condition as possible, I had sewn book covers of varying sizes with pockets for my *Ausweis* and commuter passes, because a good bit of the time spent in travel could be utilized reading.

My immediate goal now was to notify the American Consulate of my Uncle Hans' and Tante Grete's address. The Swiss lady was still part of the personnel at the Consulate, and she and the Vice-Consul were delighted that I had found a relative to stay with. They assured me that I would be on the next transport out of Germany. Greatly elated, I walked to the Alsterhaus, and dropped in to see Marion to tell her the good news. She was excited for me as well.

Everything that transpired in the next few days seemed to occur in rapid succession. As I stepped off the trolley at the *Landungsbrücken* on my way home, the St. Pauli police stood waiting to pick out every fifth woman getting off. They were randomly selected to be sent to the hospital for venereal disease examination. I had been informed of these spot checks by Irmgard's grandmother, who was one of the health inspectors in the red light district, and was relieved not to have been chosen. Upon arriving home after the ferry trip, I was surprised to find my friend Jack sitting at our kitchen table having tea with my mother. After his absence of several months, he appeared to be more handsome than I had remembered. "Well, here is our young solicitor-to-be!" he said in his clipped British accent. "I've been to the American Consulate again; soon I'll be on my way home to the States," I said excitedly to both of them. They both looked crestfallen. "Do you really want to go to uncertain surroundings, Helen?" Jack asked. My mother was near tears. "It is so grey and dismal here, no joy, no music, and I'm always hungry and tired. Anything will be an improvement!" I flung myself onto the day bed which served as our sofa. Mama poured me some tea, and pushed a box of cookies that Jack had brought along from the ship towards me. "Where is Erika?" I asked, to get the attention away from me, for I realized that my mother had spoken to Jack about my plans. Just then, my sister burst into the room, smiling. "Look what I have!" She opened up her apron, which she always wore together with her dress. "One of the ships was unloading sacks of flour near where we were playing. By chance, one of the bags broke, and Ingrid, Gerhard, and I scooped up as much as we could," she said happily. "Mama, can you make some pancakes or dumplings for us?" "I don't have any eggs," Mama answered sadly. "I will get some from the ship," Jack volunteered. He informed us that he had the watch that evening, and that he would return the following day. With that, we all shook hands, and he praised Erika for being such a great provider. I stretched my legs out on the daybed, and closed my eyes, for my knee had gotten badly infected. "Helen, Jack is very fond of you. Do you still want to go through with crossing the Atlantic alone?" Mama asked. All I could do at that moment was to pretend that I was asleep. I knew that my mother was very reluctant to have me leave the family again. However, since early childhood, I had learned to cope with being on my own, that is, to settle inner conflicts by myself. I still remember vividly, the time I sat underneath the bright light of the New York Eye, Ear, and Throat Hospital operating table for my second mastoid operation. The surgeon scrubbed up in back of me, while the nurse reassured me, "Brave little girls aren't afraid of anything." With that, I was asked to count down while the anaesthesia mask was placed over my face. When I later awoke with my head completely bandaged, I felt like Humpty Dumpty, however, I gradually began to realize that I was still alive. During the next few days in the hospital, and afterwards at home, as I slowly recovered, I thought to myself, what a marvelous sentry I have within me which tends to the miraculous healing of my body. Now, as I mused about that amazing guard, I was confident that my knee would become properly healed, and I could once again stroll without a limp. So, I fell asleep. When I woke up, my mother was sitting on a chair by the table next to the couch, reading. I saw that it was the book I had borrowed from my teacher, Frl. Schmidt. I kept it in the drawer of the kitchen cupboard, only to read it in the house, for I did not want it to be either damaged or lost while I had it in my possession. It also was the book that gave me an understanding of my own internal creativity. "Did you read The Dance of Life?" Mama asked. "It is way too complicated for me to fully understand, but is nevertheless very interesting." Of course, it was complicated for me, too, but Havelock Ellis gave me the answers to many questions and thoughts I had. It augmented the tales Papa, Uncle Hans, and their friends had told in New York City. Then she put the book down, and I knew that she was mightily trying to craft a few sage sentences to give me the facts of life. This topic she and my step-grandmother had broached several times in the past. After many awkward attempts by both of them, I remember overhearing Oma

138

saying to Mama, *"Keine Angst, Martha, Helen hat Biologie in der Schule; das ist mehr wie genug!"* As Lutherans, they were reconciled with relying on my school teachers to enlighten me. I had gotten my first period when in York, at the age of 14. Frau Huber, who was my *Pflegemutter* (foster mother), and also my career woman idol, had explained the hygiene aspects of a woman's condition by giving me a set of washable pads, for even she, as the owner of her own drugstore, could not get enough disposable supplies during and even after the war. "Now that you are a woman, don't let any man touch you inappropriately, but *Küssen ist keine Sünd'*." (Kissing is not a sin) My mother used the very same phrase, which was taken from an operetta melody, and made me smile. Mama then looked at my knee, and assured me that it was healing well. Erika came in from playing with her Neuhof pals. We had some soup, and then went to bed early. We all always tried to get as much rest as possible in order to conserve our limited energy.

"SPRUCED UP, FRESHLY shaved, and carrying a gym bag, Jack's coming," Erika announced, for she was sitting on the front steps shuffling cards, and keeping an eye down the street to the Free Harbor gate. The workers and ship crew members had to show their passes, and at random were subjected to inspection of their baggage and their persons. "How do you know that he's coming?" I called from the couch, since windows and the front door were open. "I can smell his aftershave," Erika laughed, and at that, Jack knocked on the open door and stepped into the room. Mama was preparing some carrot soup from her first harvest, and was stirring the pot. "I only could get two eggs, for the ship's cook is a Scot," he said. "Our rations aboard an English ship are not as generous as on an American steamer." With that, he opened his gym bag, which had the promised two eggs, some tea, sugar, and a beautiful bar of soap for me. I had been reading, as usual, but the book was lying on the table. "Are you reading Havelock Ellis, Helen, or is your mother?" My mother answered for me, that I had lamented at only having a copy in German, and went on at great length about how I looked forward to some day reading the book in English. Jack then volunteered that his parents had several volumes of Ellis' work in their personal libraries. "My favorite author is Joseph Conrad," I recall him saying. We all chatted amiably, then watched Erika manipulate her cards, while my mother stirred the batter to make pancakes from Erika's flour and the eggs that Jack had brought. Mama had a small amount of olive oil left from Papa's Italian seaman friend. It was a great afternoon, but we all missed Papa. Jack told us that he could tell that Papa had been a sailor by his walk. We all laughed, and I then imitated his gait. Upon seeing that, Jack thought that I was up to going for a walk.

We strolled along the Nippoldstrasse, and, as we passed the empty shell of an apartment house with the rubble pile still lying about, Jack reminded me of the tedious labor of picking, scraping, and transporting bricks to build our house. Then he praised my father's accomplishments with, "He's an exemplary Yank, one of the truly pioneer men that America is made of. I'll bet he was a good shipmate when he was at sea." As we walked towards the end of the block, we were being observed by neighbor Frau Winkler and a group of the women coming home from a shift in the fish factory. I knew that tongues would be busy with gossip. The word would spread over the peninsula like the all pervasive scent of the fish-girls. *"Die Amerikanerin mit dem schicken Englischen Schiffsoffizier,"* they whispered as we went by, and the girls threw envious glances our way. Jack seemed to be oblivious to the stares we were objects of, or otherwise simply chose to be unaffected by them. When we reached my beach near the old fishing cottages, I felt more relaxed. We sat down on the sand, and he began to tell me of the various voyages, the ships, and the different captains he had sailed with. He also stated that he was not yet certain what his future life's work would be. When there was a silence between us, I began to speak of my own plans of returning to New York City, my hope of studying law at Yale or Columbia, enjoying milkshakes at the local ice cream parlors, and joining the neighborhood free libraries my father had told me about. "I want to stroll through Central Park, go to the Roxy Theater and Radio City Music Hall, and dance at Roseland. On Sunday afternoons, I'll spend time in Yorkville's German neighborhood on 86th Street, at the Cafés Geiger and Hindenburg, and the Kleine Konditorei." I gazed out over the Elbe, and dreamt of America while Jack just looked at me. "What are some of the songs that you remember, besides Lilli Marlene," I asked Jack. I knew that every soldier, both English and American, loved the lyrics *"Vor der Kaserne"*. "There is this teenage idol named Frank Sinatra who makes all the Oxford-shoed Bobby Soxers swoon. I heard him on the BBC singing 'All, or Nothing At All' and 'I'll Be Seeing You'," Jack said. He suggested that we drop by the Neuhof *Gastwirtschaft,* where we might hear some new recordings of American music several of the local seamen may have brought along. The only songs that I was still familiar with were those of the '30s, such as "By Mir Bist Du Schein", and "The Merry-Go-Round Broke Down, before my family and I had come to Germany. Songs had always been a very important part of my life. The old German folk song that my parents had learned from their parents, *"Die Gedanken Sind Frei"* (Thoughts are free), was very meaningful to me because of the restrictions to freedom during the Hitler regime. Many song titles had been inscribed into my confirmation album as words of encouragement by my teachers and fellow students. My favorite teacher, Frl. Gertrud Schmidt, had printed the words to Martin Luther's song *"Eine Feste Burg ist unser Gott"*, which I frequently referred to for solace. It is difficult to have feelings of comfort and security when years of stress have permeated one's body, especially for a teenager who has been malnourished, and angered to be in a place that has been destroyed by the countrymen one loves. My sense of safety had long been taken from me. I only knew that I had to learn to be entirely self-sufficient. I realized how fortunate I had been to have had my parents, my sister, my teachers, and now, a friend like Jack. However, going home was all that really mattered to me at this time, and Jack realized it only too sadly. Slowly, we walked back to the housing block. We turned into the street past the Police Station. A few steps further, and the strains of "Sentimental Journey" could be heard emanating from the tavern. Jack opened the door, and held it for me to step into the smoke-filled interior. All eyes were upon us, and again I heard, *"Die Amerikanerin mit dem Engländer"*. The barflies glued their glances on Jack, while the waitress tango-slid across the floor. Jack ordered a beer for himself, and a soft drink for me. Again, he seemed oblivious to the effect he had on the women. We continued our conversation about the kinds of popular music I would be hearing in America, and listened to two or three more of the Allied "Hit List" recordings being played in the bar. We left when we started to hear the strains of "Lilli Marlene", after Jack had paid the bill and left a tip of three American cigarettes for the waitress. I hummed along as we continued our stroll back to my home, in plenty of time to avoid missing the curfew. Jack asked me to sing the words and tell him their meaning, so I imitated the songstress Marlene Dietrich with my alto voice. We arrived at the bucolic *Schrebergarten* road on which our cottage stood just as I finished. "Our ship is leaving on the morning tide," Jack said quietly. "I have the night watch on board, but this time, it will not be months of dry dock repairs before our voyage back to Hamburg." Suddenly, from out of one of the garden lots, a huge police dog pounced on me, throwing me to the ground. Jack quickly grabbed the dog's collar, and tried to pull the animal off me, but without success. As the dog continued to menace me, fortunately without biting, I grasped a handful of brush and attempted to push him away, while at the same time trying to calm him with quiet commands. I then became aware of the black-garbed ex-Gestapo man, who stood over me, laughing sadistically. He finally ordered the dog off me, and commanded Jack to return to his ship before the curfew came into effect. Jack helped me up, ignoring the scoundrel's directions. The dog now was menacing him, and the policeman threatened to arrest him: *"Ich verhafte Sie wenn Sie nicht gehen!"* I was so shaken up, that I became transfixed, but managed to whisper to Jack to inform my mother. I realized that the villain who had been responsible for my father's arrest was now after me as well. *"Was wollen Sie von mir?"* I shouted at him. He ignored my question, while the canine continued to growl threateningly at Jack and me. Slowly, we tried to walk away and reach my garden gate. Just then, the curfew siren sounded. "You are in violation of curfew!" the Neuhof enforcer called out, "that is why you are being arrested." Jack now quickly ran towards the Free Harbor gate. With the dog at my heels, the devil incarnate pushed me along. When we returned to the housing block, he went through the motions of checking each doorway in order to delay the time it took us to reach the police station, thus justifying the time of my arrest. He obviously took great delight in continuing to intimidate me as much as possible. I regarded the man as a much greater menace than the dog, who was only obeying the commands of his master. "The dog can easily throw you down again, just as he did to your father." We turned a corner, and arrived at the station, in the same block where, only an hour ago, Jack and I had heard the strains of the latest *Schlager* emanating from the tavern. The young policeman at the desk had obviously been napping, and looked up with sleepy eyes. My captor ordered me to sit in the chair by the desk. *"Ausweis, bitte!"* came the familiar command for identity papers. I threw my cellophane-covered card onto the desk in front of the officer, while he put a sheet of paper into the typewriter. Just then, footsteps were heard on the tile floor at the entrance. Jack and my mother came charging in. Jack berated my black-garbed captor in English, while my mother shouted in German. It was nearly the same dialog from both of them. The robbing of freedom from my father, and now of his daughter, both having been assaulted and brought to this station. "Helen was waylaid by you before the curfew, and was already at our garden gate," they both emphasized. "You miserable scoundrel!" Jack added. *"Sie Teufel, Sie hirnloser Ochse, mit Ihren Gastapo Methoden!"* were some of my mother's additional choice words. The young policeman behind the desk hung his head in embarrassment. "For that, you are now both also under arrest!" the enforcer shouted. Mama simply ignored his threat, and continued to curse him with words I had never heard her use. *"Das ist mir Scheissegal, Sie Rindvieh.. Der arme Hund muss so einen Idiot wie Sie folgen!"* She caught her breath, which gave Jack a chance to say firmly to both men, "The captain of my ship is aware of the situation. I am to tell you that!" My mother translated that message, while I grabbed my ID from the table, and saw the policeman slink lower behind the desk to avoid our looks of disdain. Jack quickly guided us both out of the station.

The American Hamburger comes Home

J ack bid us a hasty goodby at our garden gate, for one of his shipmates had stood the watch for him. We did not know if the captain even knew about his absence. His performance at the police station had been most effective, and my mother thanked him for helping us. "I'll be seeing you, Helen," were the last words Jack called out to me as he ran off to the Free Harbor gate to get aboard his vessel.

Mama and I hugged each other in relief. She unlocked the front door, and we found Erika huddled on the day bed with Moochie on her lap. My sister was very frightened, for she had witnessed my father's treatment by the ex-Gestapo man, and feared that my mother and I might not return. She had been crying, and was very happy to see us. We all hugged each other, and my mother set about to make us some tea. The camomile calmed us, and we climbed up to our sleeping quarters. The next day, when the mail came, I received notice from the American Consulate, signed by the Vice-Consul Francis J. Galbraith, that my passage to New York had been paid, and a boat was now scheduled to leave Bremen about July 5th, 1946. My mother was sad, for she had hoped that I really would not follow through with my plan to leave home alone. She began to cry. "What about your father? We still don't know where he is, and you won't even be able to say goodby to him!" Then she added, "And what about Jack?" That was all I could bear; I excused myself, and went for a walk. For hours, I sat on the sand near the old fishing cottages. Then, I became aware of someone watching me. Helmut was throwing pebbles into the Elbe, and I finally reacted to his distraction. "I saw you walking yesterday with your English lord," he commented sarcastically as he approached me. I did not answer. "I bet he proposed to you." I just shook my head. He sat down in the sand beside me. After a long silence, I said, "I'm leaving on July 5ᵗʰ to go home to America." "Oh," was his only comment. I started to get up to walk away. *"Ich besuche die Seemannschule, habe schon den Anfang hinter mir,"* he said. "When I get my seaman's papers, I'll be able to come to visit you." I bid him goodby, and walked briskly back to our cottage. Mama was hoeing in the garden, and Erika had helped by pulling weeds. *"Wir werden Feldsalat zu unseren Bratkatoffeln essen,"* Mama said happily. I was glad that she was no longer in a crying mood. "Can I help?" I called out. "Now, after I have already done all the weeding, she wants to help!" Erika commented. "You can wash the greens for our dinner, and put the last of the old potatoes on the hearth to boil," Mama called out. I did as I was told. "Tomorrow, I'll go into work at the law office. My knee has healed sufficiently now. I'll have to tell Herr Aschermann about my voyage home," I said to Mama and Erika as we ate our potatoes, which I had sauteed with small chunks of Spam and onions. The greens were tossed with herbs and vinegar. We enjoyed our *Abendessen.* "By the way," Erika said, "Nick-the-Greek was asking for Helen while I was sitting on the front stoop playing with the cat." "I hope you didn't encourage him to come around!" Mama said sharply. "No, I told him that Helen was either at work or at the university." I was relieved to hear that.

IT WAS A beautiful, sunny morning as I took the *Jollenführer* ferry to commute to the office on what was to be my last day at Herr Aschermann's law office. Only a few harbor workers in tattered clothes sat in the cabin enclosure while I chatted with the mate on deck, who mentioned that one of my father's friends, a Greek, had asked where I worked. "I hope you didn't tell him where!" I snapped, angrily.

Lots of paperwork had accumulated, which kept me shuttling through the mazes of bureaucratic halls. I had become quite proficient in getting the required forms stamped, signed, or court dates changed, using diplomatic flattery, for my employer's convenience. As I was about to reenter my employer's office building that late afternoon, Nick-the-Greek was standing at the entrance. He called out to me. I was highly annoyed to see him, and made it perfectly clear that I would not further tolerate his ungentleman like behavior towards me. He was carrying a package, which he proffered to me, saying, "For you pretty clothes!" I waved it off with the comment, *"Nein, danke!"*, and ducked into the building. Herr Aschermann was alone in the office. He looked very ill. His hawk-like features were more pronounced than ever, and his thin, jaundiced skin appeared taught across his hollow cheek bones, giving him a cadaverous look. His eyes gave the only sign that he was still alive. He was pleased to see me, delighted that the pile of red tape that had accumulated had been picked up, delivered, stamped, processed, and now filed by me again. Only after my briefcase had been emptied, and I had asked for his signature on several documents, did I tell him that I was to sail home to America. "Have you found out where they are holding my father?" Now he looked even more ill than before. *"Nein, noch nicht!"* I was very disappointed that he had not managed to receive any further information. He assured me that he would be in touch with my mother the minute he heard anything about my father's whereabouts. We shook hands, and he wished me good luck with my life and studies in America. *"Die Hauptsache ist, Sie bekommen Ihre drei Mahlzeiten!"* Yes, to have three meals a day, as well as peace of mind, are indeed the most essential qualities of life. I wished him all the best, especially good health, as I left the Messberg office for the last time.

I could see that Nick-the-Greek was still standing across the street, so I asked the janitor to please let me out the back way. The next few days consisted of visits to Mama's Altonauer friend Irma for the last fittings of the rayon dress and the white cotton skirt and bolero jacket. I received my passport and directions to the UNRA center in Bremen for my dormitory stay from the Hamburg American Consulate. Also, I dropped in to say goodby to Marion and her mother at the Alster Haus. We hoped and wished each other a better life. My final words of advice to her, were for her not to marry a German. We were not to cross paths again for 25 years. If I managed to bid farewell to my other friends, is a blur in my memory, like a fast speed section of an old movie.

I BRAIDED MY sister's hair on the morning we prepared to leave for the journey to Bremen. I told her the fairy tale of the *Bremer Stadtmusikanten* (Bremen Town Musicians). The donkey, the dog, the cat, and the rooster were travel companions on the way to Bremen. We laughed, and Erika said, "*Und du bist die Tillah die nach Amerika reist.*" Tillah is the heroine of an extensive ditty who travels to America with her wealthy father, and must have all of her clothing and surroundings in *lilllah* (lavender). I of course, was to travel alone, although my own favorite color also happens to be lilac. "That's right, and when I have a job, and have paid back my travel expense to Uncle Hans, I will send for you. Would you like that?" Erika was delighted at the prospect, but my mother bit her lip, and did not comment.

Bremen is Germany's second largest seaport, next to Hamburg. It had also been heavily bombed by the allied forces during the war. After a painful parting at the Bremen American Consulate, I was alone among the collected Americans from North Germany. For several days, we were given beds in a school dormitory, and received food in the cafeteria twice daily. We were assembled into classrooms, and quizzed as to our knowledge of our country's history. Army officers were our teachers and lecturers, and their main function was to remind us of our American heritage. "Where was George Washington's home? In which city did our first President take the oath of office?" they asked us. Of course, I had been to Mount Vernon, riding in the side car with my mother in my father's Harley, varooming into the estate on the Potomac. I also knew that George Washington had taken the oath of office on the premises of Federal Hall in New York City. "Did you know that the constitution of the United States was first printed in German, much to the chagrin of Benjamin Franklin, one day before it was published in English?" I posed that question to our instructor. "The largest foreign stock to settle in the USA were from Austria, Germany, Luxemburg, and Switzerland," I bragged to him who was there to test us. Many of my fellow classmates spoke very little English, had been heavily indoctrinated by the Nazi regime, and now had to be de-Nazified. My English now had acquired a somewhat British intonation, since most of my teachers had studied in England. "Our country was filled with Indians, and some of my ancestors were pioneers going west generations ago," I touted. *"Du bist eine Angeberin,"* said the girl next to me as we stood in line at the mess hall.

Her name was Margaret, and her spoof of my bragging was not really meant in a nasty way. She was to live with her uncle in St. Louis. I was delighted to make her acquaintance and also to receive the largest portions of food either of us had seen in years. At each mealtime, we would be the very first in line, waiting for the smiling soldiers assigned by the quartermaster to dispense our rations. At dinner, we had slices of Spam, Popeye-the-Sailorman's spinach, and macaroni and cheese. In between times, our teachers gave us instructions on singing our national anthem, pledging allegiance to the flag, and a general reader's digest version of citizenship indoctrination.

That evening, we were invited to attend a boxing match between the American and British amateur champions. An outdoor ring had been set up in the park adjoining the building we were housed in. I was given a ringside seat, and witnessed the event up close in which two men beat each other to a squichy mess. When the blood squirted over my way, I vowed never again to attend such an exhibition in person again. In later years, however, I became a TV boxing fan, and had the opportunity to meet several champions when I worked for a novelty company on Broadway.

The morning after the boxing event, all the American citizens that were to board our ship were transported by train directly to the Bremerhaven waterfront. Although none of us had really given much thought as to what sort of vessel would carry us back home to the States, we were all nevertheless taken aback when we caught sight of the troop ship Marine Flasher berthed at the quay side. I had arrived in Germany aboard the luxurious Presidential liner S.S. Roosevelt via Ireland, England, and France. I had been aboard many ocean liners that my father had worked on before he had been forced into the submarine repair service in Hamburg. I now beheld this gray, ugly, transport which was to be our home for the next two weeks, and felt like the Pilgrims may have upon first seeing the Mayflower. The Marine Flasher had been built in 1945 by the Kaiser Co., Inc., in Vancouver, Washington, and had first seen service in the Asian theater of war. The ship's overall length was 523 feet, with a 72 foot beam. Its gross tonnage was 12,420, and it could take 3,485 passengers. The small contingent of American citizens I was among was the first to cross the gangplank, later to be followed by hundreds of displaced persons from the concentration camps of Germany and eastern Europe. I had my violin and briefcase in one hand, and a suitcase in the other. A crewman immediately came to assist me with my suitcase. I never again allowed myself to be parted from my precious documents and instrument. My new friend Margaret and I were escorted to an A-deck cabin normally occupied by officers. Margaret was assigned to a lower berth, and I had an upper, which gave me a view through the porthole. We were both greatly pleased with the arrangement, but the two other girls sharing our cabin complained bitterly at what they felt were the miserable accommodations we would have to endure. Margaret and I were to be constantly amazed at what spoiled brats those two turned out to be. At first, we tried to humor them, but after a while, it became so exhausting to socialize with them, that we just began to ignore them. We appreciated our accommodations even more after we saw the conditions of the DPs in the crowded between decks in the bowels of the ship, where row upon row of double and triple level berths offered little privacy. In addition, whereas we enjoyed officer's dining room service, they received only two meals daily in a cafeteria style mess hall, and only had the use of communal showers and toilets. Our upper deck dining room was furnished with white linen tablecloths and napkins, and our formally attired waiter, a tall black man, handed us menus at each meal. This was the first time in my life that I had experienced close contact with a person of color, and he was greatly amused by my awkwardness. He made a particular point of showing me the contrast of pigment between the palms of his hands and the rest of his skin. During the course of the voyage, we experienced some very heavy weather, and most of the dining room passengers remained confined to their bunks, suffering from mal-de-mer. I was fortunately completely unaffected, and made certain that I never missed a meal serving. I took every opportunity to make up for the years of starvation during the war by selecting something on the menu from every available dish. "Dear me, dear me," the waiter would moan, when I alone caused him as much work as all the rest of the passengers might have, had they even been present. I immediately memorized the entire breakfast menu, beginning with orange juice, prune juice, grapefruit, oatmeal, ham and eggs, toast and jam, and coffee as well as hot chocolate. I would allow myself a full two hours to savor this marvelous repast. "You can't possibly be coming back for lunch," he would call after me, but I would briskly walk the decks to work off the meal, and faithfully arrive at my table at the ringing of the dinner bell. The astonished waiter would again bemoan his unfortunate lot. On sunny days and calm seas, when the deck was jammed with the below deck passengers, I preferred to stay in my bunk and read. When the seas were high, with waves breaking over the bow, I had the decks all to myself. Only when the captain gave orders over the loudspeaker to clear the decks, did I confine myself to my cabin. The crew were of various nationalities, and a handsome Swedish Finn with golden hair and a dazzling smile knocked on my cabin door. I was alone, reading in my bunk. He introduced himself as Walter Johnson. "I played cards with your waiter, and found out which cabin you were in," he said. "I brought you some coffee and a Danish. Mac told me that he never saw anybody enjoy food as much as you do." Before I could say thank you, he called out, "I have the evening watch. See you after that, and if you are interested, I can show you the constellations." He had nervously looked from side to side down the corridor, for the crew had been told not to fraternize with the American passengers. I closed the book I had been reading, and enjoyed the goodies that had been brought to me.

When I appeared at the dinner table that evening, the others were already seated. The waiter smiled for the first time, commenting, "Did you enjoy your coffee break? I figured that perhaps that might relieve some of my carrying load for suppertime now. Will it?" "Well," I said, "let's see, Mac. It'll have to last me all night through till tomorrow's breakfast. I'll walk the deck more than before, so I'll have to be fortified." The waiter then re-assumed his doleful expression, moaning, "Dear me, dear me, the Lord have mercy."

After dinner, Margaret and I returned to our cabin, and I told her about my afternoon visitor. "Are you going to meet him on deck?" she asked. "I don't know. First, I'm going to rest and read. I'll decide later." I fell asleep reading, and did not wake until the next morning. I was not tardy for an early breakfast, however. Mac greeted me with, "My shipmate missed you last night." "I fell asleep, and only now woke up," I answered. Afterwards, when I stepped outside, I leaned against the bulwarks, for no seating facilities are supplied on the deck of a troop ship. The weather was very mild and pleasant, and, although I never caught a glimpse of any other vessel during the entire passage, I was fortunate to observe dolphins playing around our bow wave on several occasions. One time, when I was on deck after a spell of heavy weather, I saw a young, dark haired girl about the age of my sister sitting huddled against one of the deck structures, crying. When I asked her what was the matter, she replied that she had come topsides to get some fresh air, but now did not remember how to return to her mother. I took her hand, and we descended to the lowest deck levels, searching for a familiar area. I was almost overcome with the stench of human body odors and vomit. We finally located her mother's berth, who was obviously as distressed from seasickness as from the prolonged absence of her daughter. In heavily Slavic accented German, she uttered her thanks, *"Danke, sie sind ein Engel."*

The rest of the voyage was uneventful, except for a three day storm, which extended the length of the trip several days past the usual ten day's crossing. When I spent time on deck, Walter frequently arranged to come by, and we chatted together as long as his free time permitted. As we neared the coast, and passed Montauk in the distance, he alerted me to watch for the Parachute Jump at Coney Island, which would be the first visible manmade landmark.

Every passenger stood, leaned, or was otherwise draped along the railings or bulwarks of the ship in awe of the spectacular entrance into New York Harbor. We all thrilled to the sights of the Statue of Liberty and the stalagmite skyscrapers of my Manhattan Island birthplace. The collective emotions of the passengers had permeated the atmosphere, and was felt by each in their own way. I let out a deep sigh, thinking of my parents and sister not being able to share this moment with me. I had not noticed if a pilot had come on board, but observed with fascination the procedures of the tugs nudging us into a berth at one of the midtown piers. Over the loudspeaker, the captain announced the procedure for debarkation. American citizens were to be called in alphabetical order, which barely gave me time to gather my sparse belongings. In a daze, I walked across the gangplank carrying my suitcase in one hand, and my violin and briefcase in the other. A tall, slender man wearing a grey suit and hat approached, looking at me questioningly. "Helen, is that you?" Uncle Hans asked in surprise. The last time he had seen me, I was an eight year old child. Although it is, of course, only to be expected, it always nevertheless is a shock to see how a child can grow in a period of eight years, the time I had spent in Germany. He was amazed at the change in my appearance, but I saw that he had remained very much as I remembered. As he was about to pick up my suitcase, my waiter walked up to us, still dressed in his white uniform. "You must be Helen's uncle," he said. "Dear me, dear me, she ate and she ate," he lamented. Uncle Hans laughed, took out his wallet, presented him with a $20 bill, and thanked him. No sooner had Mac disappeared, when Walter came running up to us. He shook hands with my uncle, introduced himself, and asked for permission to come and visit me. Uncle Hans was highly amused, and gave Walter his business card and directions to Courtland Avenue. In the meanwhile, the passenger processing had proceeded to the letter V, and Margaret came towards us. She had tears in her eyes, shook hands with me, and vowed to write to me as soon as she arrived in St. Louis. Uncle Hans lifted my suitcase, and as we walked off, I blew kisses to all of them, including the DP passengers I had befriended on the voyage. "Can you really play that fiddle?" one of them called after me. "Yes, would you like to hear Turkey in the Straw?" I kidded. I walked behind my uncle, who looked important, confidently dressed in his light grey suit, and the throng of people parted as he approached, and before I realized, we were out of the United States Lines pier building onto the street. As we walked along a line of waiting taxis and buses, we came to Uncle Hans' car. It was a beautiful, black limousine, and stood parked under the elevated highway facing the river. An excited wirehaired terrier within anticipated our arrival, and leaped out of the open window. Tante Grete still had his leash in her hand, so the poor animal dangled struggling at the side of the car, until Uncle Hans quickly lifted him back through the window onto my aunt's lap. I stepped back to admire the vehicle, as well as my aunt's chartreuse and white hat, which was all I could see of her at the moment. Uncle Hans deposited my belongings into the trunk, and opened a rear door for me to get into the spacious, grey velour-upholstered back seat. As I became seated, my white cotton skirt rode up, accentuating the length of my legs. Tante Grete, who had turned around, gasped in astonishment, and cried out, "Oh, my God, what a long drink of water!" My black pumps, which I had so carefully repaired, were on the verge of falling apart. The sea air of the voyage had rusted the tacks, and loosened the soles. I took them off, and found my white socks bloodied from the exposed nails. "You need a new pair of shoes," were the next words my aunt spoke to me. Her tulle hat had slid to the side of her head from the struggle with the dog, and I was forced to laugh at the sight. She looked like the heroine in a comic operetta. As if she had read my mind, she began singing, *"Tarrah, tarrah, die Helen ist da!"* She had a beautiful singing voice, and flashed her perfectly even white teeth. The dog now struggled to jump to the back to get acquainted with me. "What's his name," I asked. By this time, Uncle Hans had come around to the other side of the car, and slid into the driver's seat. "Nishi," he said, "is named after my Japanese physician friend, with whom I had been locked up in a detention center for aliens for six weeks. I had been working for the Pratt and Whitney Aircraft Engine Company when it was discovered that I was not an American citizen. Your aunt had to withdraw all of our savings to come up with enough money for bail and an attorney." "Come Nishi," I coaxed the dog, and he jumped into my lap and began licking my face. That greatly pleased my aunt and uncle, for the pooch was normally very scrappy and protective of them. Uncle Hans delayed driving off, giving me the opportunity to examine the beautiful interior of the 1929 Packard. The glass panel separating the chauffeur from the passengers had been removed, as my uncle had acquired the car from one of his wealthy customers, and now used it in his painting and decorating business. Although I was vastly impressed with the luxury of the vehicle, my aunt apologized for its age, telling me that new cars were still impossible to obtain. They had been forced to sell their previous car to scrape together additional funds for my uncle's bail money.

Before driving to their home, Uncle Hans took me on a sight seeing tour of midtown Manhattan. Although much of the city was still familiar, there were many changes. One of the sights that I most marveled at was the huge Camel cigarette sign in Times Square, with the face puffing out perfectly formed smoke rings at regular intervals. With deep satisfaction, I soaked up the sight of so many old and familiar New York landmarks, and slowly began to realize that finally, I now was actually home again.

Photos

Erich Georg Blyszus at age 17, on the way to look for his father in U.S.A.

Mama and Papa in front of Connecticut estate where they worked.

Papa in manager uniform at Gracie Square apartment complex, N.Y.C.

Papa, Mama, Helen, Amanda holding Erika in front Bethpage, L.I. house.

Papa with best friend Richard Witt and Richard's Jewish wife Hildegrad.

Papa and Mama in New York on honeymoon.

Helen and Erika just before leaving U.S.

Papa in German Army Uniform: too casual to keep superiors happy!

Hamburg Oberbau class in Frehne at the dairy of the hamlet in the Prignitz.

Marion and Ursula after WWII, 1945.

Mama and Erika alone in Hamburg 1944.

Foster mother Frau Huber with daughters in York, im Alten Land.

Helen and Ria with charge Anneliese.

Helen in front of large fruit farm estate.

Helen's merchant seaman friend Jack.

Helen as law apprentice.

WARSHIPTICKET
1-1-43

UNITED STATES LINES COMPANY

56357

AGENT

1.	2.	3.
4.	5.	6.

PASSENGER TICKET—(Not Transferrable)

DUP. Class Ship MARINE FLASHER _____ (As agreed)

Scheduled to sail JULY 5th _____ (Passenger to be advised) 19 46

At _____ (Not known) From Pier _____ (Passenger to be advised)

FROM BREMEN (As agreed) TO NEW YORK (As agreed)

NAMES OF PASSENGERS (This Passage is subject to terms printed, typed, stamped, or written below and on back of all pages)	Sex	Age	Room	Berth	Ocean Fare $	Taxes Collected
BLESCUS, HELEN	F	16	A 19	4	200.-	

_1_ Adults, _____ Children, _____ Quarters, _____ Infants, _____ Servants.

Issued at Bremen

Helen

Date 7/2/46

and issued in lieu
of Ord. #21

TOTAL OCEAN FARE $ 200

TAX USL

TAX

TOTAL AMOUNT RECEIVED $

Ticket from the United States Lines Co. for passage on the Marine
Flasher from Bremen to New York, July 5, 1946.

IN REPLY REFER TO
FILE NO.

THE FOREIGN SERVICE
OF THE
UNITED STATES OF AMERICA

DEPARTMENT OF STATE

American Consulate General
Hamburg, June 22, 1946

Miss Helen M. Marcus,
Nikolausstr. Harzelle 175a,
Harburg-Wilhelmsburg.

Madam:

Notice has been received from the United States Lines in Bremen that your passage to the United States has been paid.

A boat is now scheduled to leave Bremen about July 5th. If you will report to the American Consulate in Bremen, 15 Kurfürstenallee, by June 30th with your passport, your accommodations on the boat and for the period before the sailing will be arranged. The next sailing will be approximately July 16.

Very truly yours,

For the American Consul General:

Francis J. Goldsmith,
American Vice Consul.

Notification of travel arrangements from U.S. Consul, June 22, 1946.

Der
Die **Schüler(in)** ..... *Heller Esther* ....

hat von ..*18.8.*... bis ..*7.9.43*... die ......*Albert*........*Schule*

in Reichenbach besucht.

    Führung: ....

    Fleiß: ....

    Mitarbeit: ....

    Versäumnisse: ....

Reichenbach i.V., den ....*7.9.*....*1943* ....
                                Rektor

Helen's attendance record at the Albert Schule in Reichenbach i.V., 9/43, with swastika stamp.

Erika in front of the Neuhof House we all built of materials salvaged from bombed ruins.

View of Hamburg after the July 1943 bombing, taken from the Michaeliskirche tower. Photo courtesy: Bildarchiv Preussischer Kulturbesitz

Fire and Army brigade cleaning up at the corner of Bergstrasse after June 1944 air raid.
Photo courtesy: Bildarchiv Preussischer Kulturbesitz

Townspeople carrying on amidst rubble after another Hamburg air raid.
Photo courtesy: Bildarchiv Preussischer Kulturbesitz

Other books by Helen H. Buchholtz:

American Hamburger: An American Girl in Nazi Germany

Order Form

To order additional copies, fill out this form and send it along with your check or money order to: Helen Buchholtz, 79 Clubhouse Dr., Palm Coast, FL 32137
Cost per copy $13.95 plus $2.50 P&H.

Ship _____ copies of *Another Dance of Life* to:

Name_____

Address:_____

City/State/Zip:_____

❏   **Check box for signed copy**

Please tell us how you found out about this book.

☐ **Friend**   ☐**Internet**
☐ **Book Store**   ☐**Radio**
☐ **Newspaper**   ☐ **Magazine**
☐ **Other _____**